THE WORLD ACCORDING TO SALLY

The Dream:
"Ever since I was a little girl, I wanted to be on radio. In my fantasies I was a voice on the airwaves who could hold listeners spellbound with the power of words."

The Philosophy:
"I'm trying to reach one person. There isn't a crowd out there. There's just one other human being and we're trying to figure out life together."

The Lean Years:
"If you've lost your job, with no prospects in sight, there's only one way to deal with it. Go broke in style."

The Celebrities:
"Warren Beatty, whose theatrical talent is underrated, is in too much of a hurry to be sexy. He tries too hard."

"Ann Miller, the actress and dancer with the fabulous legs, has one of the most self-deprecating and charming senses of humor of anybody in show business."

"F. Lee Bailey, the famous trial lawyer, is terribly intimidating, and I'm not easily cowed."

The Fame:
"It's opened doors to the hearts of people: the famous and infamous. Through them I've found success. Unconventional success."

P9-APJ-199

SALLY

UNCONVENTIONAL SUCCESS

SALLY JESSY RAPHAËL

WITH PAM PROCTOR

ST. MARTIN'S PAPERBACKS

Grateful acknowledgment for permission to use the photograph of Sally Jessy Raphaël with Emmy is made to Joyce Ravid. All rights reserved.

Published by arrangement with William Morrow and Company, Inc.

SALLY: UNCONVENTIONAL SUCCESS

Library of Congress Catalog Card Number: 89-13258

ISBN: 0-312-92522-0

Printed in the United States of America

William Morrow edition published 1990
St. Martin's Paperbacks edition/November 1991

10 9 8 7 6 5 4 3 2 1

To
Karl Soderlund   Burt Dubrow
Dede and my children

ACKNOWLEDGMENTS

I acknowledge, above all, Pam Proctor, my co-author, who pushed me to finish this project; and Bill Adler, who introduced me to the people at William Morrow, especially my editor, Lisa Drew and her assistant, Bob Shuman.

Then I acknowledge Multimedia, especially Walter Bartlett, Peter Lund, and Tom Shannon; my producers Kari Sagin, Linda Finnell, Alex Williamson, Donna Benner, Richard Penna, Cindy Schneider; and all my TV staff. I also wish to acknowledge the ABC Radio Network: Aaron Daniels, Maurice Tunick, Dave Rimmer, and Toby Miller.

I'm grateful for the support of my family and friends, including Steve Cortez, Jay Van Vechten, Harriet Norris, Ron Kapon, Mimi Shachat, and Alan Harris.

Finally, I'm indebted to you, who watch and listen and care.

CONTENTS

CHAPTER ONE

Gambling on Life

THE SCENE was straight out of Hemingway.

There was a steamy tropical hotel, where I sat languidly at the bar, sipping a drink with a bunch of foreign correspondents who were hanging around waiting for something to happen. Among them were some pretty good reporters who went on to become famous and win prizes. But I wouldn't remember their names. Even back then, in the early sixties, I wasn't into remembering names. I just wanted to earn some money.

At the time I was a young mother living in Puerto Rico, and I had taken a brief assignment to cover an uprising in Santo Domingo as a wire service reporter. There was a part of me, as one of the only women in this world of men, that kind of enjoyed the drinking and the big boy talk and all that. But I definitely didn't want to mess with any kind of war or serious trouble.

As we sat at the bar trading stories, a photographer rushed in to announce that he had found some action. Nobody jumped. We knew it made no sense for all of us to leave the comfort of the bar and go traipsing about the countryside in search of a story.

So we usually drew lots to see who would go take a look at the situation and report back to the rest of us. We'd all rewrite our representative's story a bit and send off variations of the same account to the newspapers or wire services.

This time was my turn. "Just follow me," said the photographer.

We raced through the sultry streets of Santo Domingo, looking for a revolution. I didn't see anything that resembled an uprising—at least not until we turned a corner into a side street.

There, in front of me, was a fourteen-karat genuine dead body.

"That's really a dead person," I thought. "These people could be *serious.*"

If I had had any inkling that things were going to get messy, I might have changed my mind about going to Santo Domingo. I mean, for me, it could be a stupid way to earn some money! I would much rather have been back in Puerto Rico with the kids. I never saw myself as Margaret Bourke-White, decked out in khaki, trying to dig up hard-to-find facts to keep the world informed. I didn't mind *entertaining* the world or enlightening it. But when my skin was at stake, *that* was another matter. Especially if dead bodies were involved.

As it turned out, I didn't have much time for contemplation. The photographer was already hard at work and asked for my help.

"Okay, the lighting here is *very* bad," he said. "I can't take the picture here. We've got to drag him out into the sun." For the next few blocks I dragged the body around here and there and posed it in various locations and positions, while my colleague took pictures from every conceivable angle. First we propped him up. Then we laid him down. Next we moved him to a doorstep. *Finally* the photographer was satisfied, and he madly clicked away.

"These photographers are crazy," I thought.

It's a good thing I don't remember his name because a year later his photo of the dead body won some national award for the best foreign war photograph of the year. It was exhibited all over the place—and still is. I see it occasionally in books of the best press photographs.

As for me, I didn't even get a credit. Yet I was the one who had dragged and arranged the body for the prizewinning pose.

Why was I willing to risk my neck in Santo Domingo? In a way, in a capsule form, that's the story of my life. I'm a gambler at heart, a chronic, incurable risk taker. In this situation I was ready to take a risk in downtown Santo Domingo simply to get the practical reward, a few bucks.

But there was more to it than that. In a funny way, dragging that body around carried its own reward. Let's face it, how many times have you found yourself in a situation like that? Never, right? Well, I had never been in a situation like that either, but while I was in the role of fearless overseas reporter, I was going to play it for all it was worth. That day, for a brief moment, I became a character in a real-life novel, caught up in a series of events that were almost too extraordinary to be true.

The way I see it, much of life contains the opportunity for such gambles. At the very least the gambles I've taken have been doorways to adventure. At the most they've held out the possibility of fame and fortune.

So I've tried to approach every twist and turn in my life with what some might call reckless optimism. Like any true gambler, deep down I know that someday my number has to come up a winner.

CHAPTER TWO

Puerto Rican Paradise:
Early Lessons in the Art
of Risk Taking

I ALWAYS WANTED to try to be all that I could be. I think that hunger is born in you.

That's why I took what was probably the biggest gamble of my life in Puerto Rico. I simply made up my mind to divorce my husband and team up with the one person, besides my mother and kids, who believed in me and dreamed my dreams: Karl Soderlund, the man who had hired me to do an interview show on radio in San Juan.

Perhaps it wasn't Karl but the racetrack that signaled the need for a change. I had married young, and in those days I had a radio show that came on after a local report on the track. Two wonderful New Yorkers, Dan and Mary, did the show. They had colorful Brooklyn accents, and I found them absolutely delightful.

Off the air they introduced me to the people who managed and bought the horses, and that opened up a whole new world for me. I'll have to admit that there was something nice about being a young and not unpretty woman who was off work in the morning with nothing to do with the rest of her day but go to the races. And so that's exactly what I did.

At the time there were two small racetracks in San Juan. It was before the big track, El Comandante, was built, and to be truthful, the races were not as honestly run as they might have been. Now, of course, the San Juan Racing Sports Administration is in charge, and I'm sure it runs a very nice operation. But back then the racing scene was wide open, and someone always knew who was going to win. Dan and Mary were among the cognoscenti, and every day they gave me a hot tip—a *really* hot tip.

Every morning, after my radio show was finished, I'd head for the track with my two little girls, Allison and Andrea, and place a two- or three-dollar bet on whatever horse Dan and Mary had advised. Always the horse came in as they predicted.

Later I found out that not everybody who goes to the track knows who's going to win, and it almost killed my interest in horse racing. But at the time I was blissfully unaware of what I was doing. I was either terribly stupid or terribly conservative because I never really bet more than two or three dollars at a time on an absolutely sure thing. As a result, I never really won big—just consistently.

My husband never quite figured out that we were not living on the four thousand dollars he made a year from his advertising business. We probably doubled his earnings with my racetrack winnings. There was no way, though, that I could tell him what I did with my day. It was bad enough, from his point of view, that I was dragging the kids to a radio station every morning for a measly two-dollar-a-day broadcasting job. But at least he lived under the illusion that after my show I shopped and cooked and puttered around our small one-bedroom apartment like other wives. In any event I couldn't tell him what I was doing with the two dollars a day I earned at the station.

But one Christmas my bubble burst. Somehow I had convinced him to come with me for a nice family outing at the track. There was a horse running that day named— believe it or not—Santa Jesse, which was a hundred to one shot. But I had the Dan and Mary inside line, so I handed my husband fifty dollars and asked him to place the bet.

"You're betting on Santa Jesse?" he said, convinced I had lost my marbles.

"It's my name," I said. "Come on, it's two days before Christmas. Let's have some fun."

Being a conservative sort, he took it upon himself to save me my fifty dollars as a good husband should. He walked up to the window and, without telling me, didn't bet a nickel.

Santa Jesse came out of that gate more juiced than a sprinter on steroids. He proceeded to run around the track faster than any horse has ever run. It was incredible! He raced over the finish line and actually dropped dead. I have never seen another horse drop dead after the finish line, but such was racing in Puerto Rico in those days.

In the excitement of the moment I turned to my husband and cried, "We've won! Isn't it wonderful! Merry Christmas, darling!"

The way he looked at me, I knew that our marriage had gone the way of Santa Jesse.

Did I really want the power in my life to be in someone else's hands? The answer was no, and I determined from that moment on that I needed to live more on my own terms.

Luckily Karl Soderlund understood what made me tick, and together we forged a new life of adventure and crazy risk taking that has been the secret of our togetherness for nearly twenty-five years.

Life in Puerto Rico in the sixties was a constant round of discovery. With Karl acting as my agent, program director, and chief cheerleader, I pushed myself to learn as much as I could about broadcasting.

San Juan was an interviewer's dream. Since Cuba was closed to tourists, they all came to Puerto Rico. Night life was in its heyday, and there was a steady stream of stars coming to the island to perform at the hotels. I'd grab them for my radio show or turn up at the hotels to watch their acts and glean whatever I could about performing. Many of them also taught me lessons about life that have shaped me to this day.

Take Joe Louis, for example. We were sitting around his hotel one rainy afternoon after an interview when I suddenly blurted out, "Joe, can you teach me how to box?"

The heavyweight champion of the world didn't even flinch at the absurd suggestion. He was a gentle, sweet man, and when a flyweight of a woman asked to learn how to box, he took the request seriously.

He immediately stood up and proceeded to give me pointers on how to handle myself in the ring.

Now, I've always believed that you should be as much of a champion as you can be, and I preach that on my radio show every night of the week, but as Joe Louis began working with me on boxing, I felt that you really *can* be all you can be. Although I may not have the physical stuff to be the heavyweight champion of the world, the truth is I could feel closer to it than I ever dreamed possible.

Years later I was put to the test. I was doing my television show in St. Louis, and we decided to do a show on professional boxers—*female* boxers. Believe it or not, there are actually seventy-two of them in the world. These women are not like mud wrestlers. The boxers are serious.

At any rate, several of them came on the show, and we set up a boxing ring on the set and got ready to do a boxing routine. The idea was for me to work out with a female boxer named Tiger, who's tops in the business.

Well, I hopped into the ring with my red satin boxing shorts, and when the bell rang, I let loose. I went after her with an instinct that came from deep inside. For a moment I forgot I was a television talk show host. I was a demon.

In my mind I flashed back two decades earlier to that meeting with Joe Louis. Suddenly I knew how to hold my hands, and I went for it.

Tiger looked stunned. "Where the hell is this coming from?" she muttered, and easily defended herself from my attack. But the more she pulled back, the more I went at her. It went on for about a minute, and luckily for me, Tiger was pulling punches. Frankly, if she had not had the control of a professional boxer, I would have been dead. Probably she could have unleashed one real punch, and it would have been over.

But I wasn't thinking about anything but the fight. Some sort of primal instinct took over. It was the same kind of instinct that happens to a mother when she sees her child in the way of an oncoming car. The adrenaline rises, and you say to yourself, "I can do this. I can kill if I want to. I'm wearing the right gloves. Go for it."

If Joe Louis taught me about the art of the possible, an experience I had with Jackie Mason was a harbinger of my hard times ahead as a female broadcaster. Jackie, of course, is now a big, big star with his name in lights after his success on Broadway in *The World According to Me*. But even back then, when he was a not-very-famous stand-up comic playing the clubs, he operated as though he had the world in his hands.

It was early in the morning on a local radio show in Puerto Rico, and like a lot of people before him, Jackie didn't really want to be there. But he did want the publicity for his nightclub act, so he sat down in the sound booth ready to make the best of it. When the red light went on, we were on the air. At the time I was in my early twenties and not very secure in my role as an interviewer, but I always plunged ahead with my questions as though I really knew what I was doing.

We bantered back and forth, and I found myself captivated by the man's comic genius. I was just beginning to feel that the interview was going pretty well when all of a sudden he reached under my sweater, unhooked my bra, and cupped my breasts in his hands.

I was repelled. I was shocked. I was scared. I was dumbfounded. But there was absolutely nothing I could do about it but try to get the interview over as fast as I could. I was on live radio, after all, and the listening audience didn't have a clue what was happening to me. What's more, I had a job I wanted to keep. Meanwhile, as I sat there in horror, Jackie was laughing and the men in the control room were laughing with him.

That was a kind of crude taste of what life could be like for a female broadcaster. However, I have to say that in the years since, in all the stations I have worked on, and with the hundreds of people that I have met, I have never been asked for any sexual favors. Aside from the incident with Jackie Mason, I have never had a pass made at me, nor have I ever had anyone insinuate that I should be "nice" to him in return for a job. I do believe that these things happen, but only because other people have told me so, not because I've been confronted with them.

What my experience with Jackie Mason taught me, though, was that there is little that is glamorous about the "glamorous" world of broadcasting. Also, you have to expect the unexpected and be constantly ready to roll with the punches.

If I ever had any illusions about broadcasting, they have been thoroughly dispelled. You discover quickly that to stay in this business, you have to put more than your intellectual skills on the line. Your ego and even your very person can be challenged at every turn, and you have to learn how to take it—or fight back.

Fortunately, though, most of us have more going for us than being someone's sweater girl. My show had become the most popular daytime show in San Juan, and I was riding the crest of a wave.

Karl was selling advertising spots like crazy, and we were bringing in more money than we would see for a long, long time. He had struck a deal with the station's owner to split the profits on any commercial time he sold. Since Karl's a master salesman, it meant that for a time, at least, we were on easy street.

So we lived a good life. For us that means four things: travel, broadcasting, shopping, and going into business, not necessarily in that order.

For starters, there was the art gallery we bought for my mother, Dede, to give her something to do. My mother was a wonderful artist, who as a young woman had gone to the Art Institute of Chicago to study painting. She continued to paint as I was growing up, and the house was always filled with the wonderfully pungent smell of her oils.

What's more, Mother and I had a powerful relationship, and it was only natural that she would figure into our lives and our plans in a big way. What we didn't realize at the time was that along with having a terrific talent, Dede was also incredibly eccentric.

In searching for a gallery to buy, I turned to an expatriate American named Bob Smith, alias Don Roberto. He owned two galleries: one in Old San Juan and one in the Sheraton Hotel. But he was getting tired of running both of them, and when he confided to me one day that he wanted to sell, I jumped at the chance.

For twenty-five hundred dollars, we bought a gallery where Mother could sell the works of local painters. All of us threw ourselves into the venture. To run a gallery correctly, you have to find painters and nurture them along. You give them cocktail parties and exhibitions and promote their works all over town. This takes a tremendous amount of work to do right, and for about a year we ran it straight.

But then it occurred to Mother that running a gallery this way was really a lot of trouble. The artists were basically a pain in the neck, not to mention the fact that she didn't think much of their work.

So she did what came naturally: She simply invented a new Puerto Rican artist named Juan Asia (pronounced "Wanna Seeya") and did all the paintings herself. She even went so far as to create a background history for this new artistic discovery.

The remarkable thing was that Juan Asia's works sold like crazy. Mother wasn't one to rest on her laurels, and in the wake of her success she figured that if one fictitious artist worked, two or three ought to do even better. So she invented a few more, and before long she was knocking out paintings for five "artists" in a variety of styles. That wasn't hard to do for a schooled artist. Juan Asia was the primitive; then there was a modernist and a traditionalist and so on.

Our gallery carried those artists on a permanent basis, along with the works of some legitimate artists as well. The really scary thing is that two of her paintings were sold to very reputable art galleries, and a couple of them now hang in museums in California and Massachusetts.

"Someday this is all going to catch up to us," I said to Karl.

It hasn't yet.

My only regret is that I don't have more of her paintings. Not one Juan Asia! The only other tangible legacy we have from that period in our lives is a fabulous collection of Puerto Rican Santos, primitive folk art figures of saints carved by hand in the nineteenth century, which we started amassing with a vengeance.

When we weren't collecting, or running the gallery, or doing the radio show, we were busy trying to keep our family life in some semblance of order. Our household was then, as it is now, a hodgepodge of kids and animals. There were my little girls, Allison and Andrea; our twelve-year-old newspaperboy, Robbie, who moved in with us one day and stayed virtually for the rest of his life; and our cat, Cynthia Schnee, whom we had rescued from the Schnee hot dog factory in San Juan.

Add to this mélange the fact that I never, ever intended to be anything but a career woman, and you've got problems. The glue that made the whole thing work was a remarkable old woman named Reencarnación Juarbe.

Reencarnación was a small, dark, wizened grandmother who was our housekeeper for many years. She had a laugh that was like a cackle and a wonderful store of Puerto Rican nursery rhymes that she recited endlessly. I still remember silly nonsense ditties like *"Arroz con leche me quiere casar con una viudita de la capital."* That translates roughly as "Rice and milk I want to marry a widow from the capital." That just about makes as much sense as any of us had in those days.

Reencarnación was very, very motherly and domestic; that was a good thing because I didn't fit either description. To me, homemaking was simply one of the roles I found repetitive. Periodically, though, I'd throw myself into the homemaker role to see what new and exciting adventures would result.

One day, for example, I looked around the house and realized that something was missing from our lives. What was missing was elegance. The bald truth was, we lived like peasants when we should have been living like *patrones.*

What triggered my sudden interest in such things was *Vogue* magazine. I had been leafing through an old issue and had come upon a feature on gracious living. There, in a luxurious home, was a person I like to call Mrs. Buff Orffington. That's my nickname for every rich woman. In the magazine "Mrs. Buff Orffington" was seated at her linen-draped dining-room table, which was set with gorgeous china and crystal. Not only that, but someone was serving the meal to her.

I don't know why, but I zeroed in on this elegant scene and realized in a blinding flash that our dining habits were all *wrong*. Somebody should be serving our meals to us! But the first problem was, we didn't even have a proper table. So, like a society shark in a feeding frenzy, I set out to live à la *Vogue* in the style to which I thought I should be accustomed.

First we bought a dining-room table. Then we started collecting china and crystal like crazy. The place to go for such things in those days was St. Thomas, a genuine free port that was a half hour away by plane. Two or three times a week we'd go to the airport and hitch a ride on someone's plane. Or we'd travel on commercial airlines that bought ad spots on our radio show.

Once in St. Thomas, we made a beeline for a fabulous little china shop owned by Claude Caron, the father of actress Leslie Caron. Next to Noel Coward, he was my idea of the definitive gentleman. What I also liked about him was that he owned a Citroën—one of those funny little cars you see in all the French movies. Every year he'd go to France and buy a new Citroën. We got to know him so well that pretty soon we worked out a deal to buy his used cars.

Thanks to Claude, we loaded up on china and crystal and were all set to live like "Mrs. Buff Orffington" when I realized that an elegant table wasn't enough. We still had to have someone to serve our meals to us. It couldn't be Karl because he had to sit at the head of the table. Obviously Reencarnación would have to learn to serve.

Our style up to then had been very democratic. Usually at meals Reencarnación would throw the food at us and then sit down and eat as part of the family. As a result, it was a difficult job for me to convince her that she should bring our food around and eat hers someplace else. She gave it a dry run a few times and failed miserably. Some days she wanted to eat in the kitchen; other days she'd forget and just sit down with us.

To underscore her new role, I decided to buy her a maid's outfit, at no less a place than Bergdorf Goodman in New York City. I thought it was the grandest store I had ever seen, and in those days it had a department where you could outfit your servants. Since I was about Reencarnación's size, I tried on several lovely black silk outfits with white aprons and cuffs, and I imagined how fabulous Reencarnación would look in them.

It never worked. No matter how hard she tried, she couldn't remember to put both cuffs on, or she couldn't get the hat right on her hair, or she'd wear the apron around her shoulders. I tried talking to her about it, but somehow it took too much energy to try to sort it out.

Despite Reencarnación's resistance, I was still determined to take one more stab at living like "Mrs. Buff Orffington." In my mind, I could picture a wonderful dinner party at my home, with good friends around an elegantly appointed table and Reencarnación serving the meal.

I invited a bunch of friends to what turned out to be my last gasp as a society matron. With the table set elegantly and everything else in order, Reencarnación came in perfectly attired in her maid's uniform—and wearing bright red sneakers.

Instead of crawling under the table in embarrassment, I became fascinated watching her pad around the dining room in that fire engine red footwear. I also realized this was a sign that this phase of my life was over—forever. No matter how hard I tried, I just wasn't cut out to live like the beautiful people, and I never have.

What was more up our alley was throwing ourselves into trying to "do good." Somehow Karl and I were always getting involved in causes. It comes naturally to me to promote things I believe in, and my radio show often became the vehicle to inspire others to join in a worthwhile task.

First, there was the Volunteer Library League. We all take public libraries for granted. I was brought up using the public library in Scarsdale, New York, and I was sure everyone had access to such free libraries. Then one day on the way to Old San Juan I came across a dilapidated old building that housed the remains of what was supposed to be Puerto Rico's public library.

Andrew Carnegie had donated money to set up libraries in the United States, and Puerto Rico had received its share. The government built the building and stocked it with a few books, but there was no money left to keep the building functioning and buy new volumes.

The old Carnegie building was lovely; but the roof leaked, and few people ever went inside. Then it dawned on a bunch of us that we could try to create a new library system. About twenty of us got together and asked every person we knew to donate English-language books. We also got someone to give us a large shed where we could store the books. Eventually the floor of the shed was covered with piles of books on different subjects.

Of course, none of us knew anything about starting a library. But then one woman got a book on the Dewey decimal system, and we were off on a cataloging spree. After we had got the books in order, we opened the library's doors three times a week, with a crew of volunteers manning it.

Little by little people started coming and taking out books, and for the first time the adults and children on the island could see how a library worked. Since then our fledgling library has been turned over to the government of Puerto Rico, and the Department of Public Instruction now runs a very substantial public library system.

Our next venture in do-gooding was saving lost animals. There were about fifty thousand homeless dogs and cats in Puerto Rico back then and a very small devoted bunch of fuddy-duddies who had the most woebegone animal shelter you've ever seen. So Karl and I decided that if we didn't do something to help those animals, we would become part of the problem. We joined forces with this little bunch of ragtag animal lovers and determined not only to help the animal problem but to solve it.

That's what brought me in contact with Cleveland Amory. I had read about this American writer, a Boston Brahmin who wrote books on high society. He was a chronicler of the elite who also had a reputation as an ardent animal lover. Once I learned of his pedigree, I wrote to him to enlist his help in our cause. He immediately responded, suggesting that the next time I was in New York I should call him. We met not long after around the block from his apartment, at the Miyako restaurant, which was one of the first Japanese restaurants in the city. I had expected a rather meek, fey sort of person. Instead, I was bowled over. Cleveland is very large and commanding. He looked as if he should be out owning and running corporations and moving mountains—certainly not taking care of pussycats.

From that meeting onward Cleveland put his considerable weight behind helping the homeless animals in Puerto Rico. He drummed up support in the States among the good ladies in the Humane Society. And at his own expense he traveled to San Juan to talk some society matrons into donating money to establish a Humane Society on the island.

But he did even more. He gave us the name of a gentleman, whom I will not name, who turned out to have some rather shady connections. He was truly a fat cat, though, and made an enormous donation to our cause. That money enabled us to set up both a permanent shelter and a mobile shelter for the stray dogs and cats in San Juan.

Cleveland, of course, has done more for cats than any person alive. People even call him in the middle of the night to rescue felines from New York City drains. It was on one such rescue mission that he met the cat that became the focal point for his bestselling book *The Cat Who Came for Christmas.*

My most vivid memory of Cleveland, though, has to do with bigger animals—bulls. Puerto Rico had decided to introduce bullfighting, both to celebrate its Spanish heritage and to bring in big bucks from mainland tourists. When I told Cleveland of the plan, he was incensed and insisted on attending one of the first bullfights.

I should have known that something was going to happen. After all, here's a man who has gone to the North Pole to save the seals and to the Pacific to save the whales. He's done public relations for the coyote, and he's even tried to upgrade the image of the wolf. It should have been clear that bulls were to be his next cause célèbre.

Cleveland looked uncomfortable from the moment he took his seat, but when the picadors started poking the bull with their pics, he rolled into action. Before I knew it, this enormous American man, who was not very agile, had leaped out of his seat and jumped into the ring. He grabbed the pic out of a startled picador's hands and started poking the thing in the man's rump.

All hell broke loose. The crowd yelled. The picadors screamed. People started climbing out of the stands.

"Come on, let's get out of here!" Karl said to me. With that we ran over the benches, sprinted down the field, and grabbed Cleveland. The three of us got out of there with a crowd of people from the stadium chasing us.

The good news is that we got out alive, and so did the bulls. What's more, bullfighting never quite took hold in San Juan.

Still, being chased by a crowd out of a San Juan bullring was only part of what made our lives in Puerto Rico exciting. Even more important was the very real feeling I had that through my position on radio I had the power to make a difference in this small tropical world.

I never felt more strongly about that role than after a particularly poignant experience I had at Christmas. One day in December I was approached by a soft-spoken, mild-mannered man who looked to be about sixty. He explained that far from San Juan, on the other side of the island where my radio show didn't even reach, was a poor little village called Castañer, where he worked as a lab technician in a Brethren hospital.

The man explained that the people of the village lived in shacks and earned an average of about four hundred dollars a year. By the time they spent all their money for food and shelter, they had none left over to buy their children gifts for Epiphany, known as Three Kings' Day. To the people of the village, this was a very great tragedy, because in most of Latin America it's Epiphany, not Christmas Day, that is the time for gift giving. He was coming to me, he said, to help him get gifts for the children.

"What do you do with the gifts?" I asked.

"Generally two doctors from the hospital and I dress up as the three kings and distribute what few gifts we have," he said.

There was something about the plaintive quality of his appeal and the intensity of his concern for these villagers that moved me deeply. So we set about to make Castañer one of our projects. With the blessing of our station manager, Art Merrill, we announced the need for gifts over the radio and told everyone we could about our plan.

Gradually gifts started rolling in, but as the time drew close to Epiphany, we realized we still needed more. There were several hundred children in the little village, and we didn't want any to go without a present. So we appealed for anything that people could spare; even salt and pepper shakers were okay with us—anything that could be wrapped. Before long we had to clear a room at the station where volunteers could come in and wrap.

We wrapped, and we wrapped. At night I'd bring the packages home and wrap some more. It was hard to explain to my own children that we were going to give these gifts away, but we did it.

Epiphany was upon us. Just after New Year's we piled

all the presents in a Jeep and headed to the hospital of the Brethren in Castañer, a four-hour car trip from San Juan. On the eve of Epiphany, we put on terry-cloth bathrobes, our version of a "king's raiment," and darkened our faces with chalk to try to make ourselves look as much like the Middle Eastern kings as possible. Then Karl, Art Merrill, the lab technician, and I got on horses and rode out to the village.

It was a night perhaps much like that first Christmas in Bethlehem. In the western part of Puerto Rico the mountains are completely unspoiled, and as we climbed up the crest of the hillside, we almost seemed to touch the stars. From six in the evening until four in the morning, we rode up and down the countryside, followed by a Jeep stacked high with gifts.

As we went along, the children heard the horses' hoofbeats and threw open their shutters. When they saw the kings, they came running out of their little *casetas* and stood absolutely wide-eyed with wonder at the sight. Then they squealed with joy as we reached into a bag and pulled out a gift.

In a strange way, that starry night was the closest I've ever felt to God. It was my personal epiphany, a glimmer of the light that love brings into the world.

But God's love shone even more brightly in Castañer than anyone could have imagined. You see, the man who brought this magical night into being for those poor children—the very man who had come to see me with his humble request—was Nathan Leopold, who bore one of the most infamous names in American crime.

It was Leopold, who, in 1924 as a nineteen-year-old graduate student at the University of Chicago, had been accused and convicted along with his friend Richard Loeb of kidnapping and murdering a teenaged boy. The two youths, both sons of millionaires, had committed the crime for a paltry ten thousand dollars' ransom and the sheer thrill of it all.

Spared from hanging by the adeptness of defense attorney Clarence Darrow, Leopold was sentenced to life imprisonment. While in prison in Illinois, Leopold had educated himself in many languages and had gotten numerous degrees by correspondence. In his later years he was freed on parole in Puerto Rico, where he married a wonderful woman named Trudy, and worked as a hospital lab technician in this tiny village in the Puerto Rican mountains.

There, in Castañer, this soft-spoken Jewish man lived out his life helping the poor. And on the night of Epiphany, he was one of the kings bearing gifts to the Christ Child.

For the next three or four years we helped Nate Leopold gather gifts and distribute them among the children. But starry nights in the mountains weren't enough to hold us to Puerto Rico, where my broadcasting career was taking a fast downhill turn.

I walked into the station one day to discover that it was no longer an English-language station. Overnight my boss, Don Alfredo, a real old-fashioned land baron type who seemingly owned half the island, had converted the station to Spanish-language programming. I spoke good Spanish, of course, but my stock-in-trade was a talk show —in English.

Abruptly my Puerto Rican radio career came to an end. I was a broadcaster without a broadcast, and for Karl and me, it looked like paradise had been lost.

CHAPTER THREE

Going Broke in Style

IF YOU'VE LOST YOUR JOB, with no prospects in sight, there's only one way to deal with it. Go broke in style.

That's how Karl and I ended up sitting on the veranda of Haiti's Grand Hotel Oloffson, waiting to interview President François "Papa Doc" Duvalier. With my broadcast career finished in Puerto Rico, I had latched on to a temporary stint as a wire service reporter. Among other things, I also hoped to get a scoop and tape a radio interview to sell in the States. Here, I thought, in Port-au-Prince, I would make a few bucks and get my big break. And at the very least I'd have a good time.

I had already gone through the process of submitting a list of questions, which the infamous dictator's staff had approved. But when we arrived in Haiti, the interview that had been a sure thing dissolved. Papa Doc had taken ill, and all we could do was hang around the hotel and wait for his health to improve miraculously.

It wasn't a bad way to kill time. After all, the colorful Victorian hotel, one of the most famous in the Caribbean, had been a favorite haunt of the likes of Noel Coward and John Gielgud. Graham Greene had put it on the map in his book *The Comedians* just a few years earlier.

What made our wait for Papa Doc even more exciting,

though, was the hint of intrigue. "Be careful what you say in your room," the wire service chief had warned me. "It's probably bugged."

Karl and I thought the whole thing was very quaint and theatrical, despite the fact that there was murder and mayhem under our very noses. The Tontons Macoute, the fearsome secret police, had the rest of the country terrorized, but to us Haiti was a lark. We developed our own sign language to use in the room. And when we tired of making faces and using gestures, we spent the rest of the time either sipping hibiscus rum on the veranda or learning white-magic spells from the locals. Except for the bright pastel-colored buildings, the whole city could have been the set of a western movie.

After about a week, we finally got to interview Papa Doc. On the appointed day, we were escorted into his office by his bodyguards. The president, looking tired and sickly, came into the room dressed in his robe. He sat down behind the desk, and with my tape recorder rolling, I asked the first question.

He answered in French, even though he could speak English fluently.

I asked the second question, and again, he answered in French.

"Sir," I protested. "This is for an English-language radio station."

"I'm tired," Papa Doc said with a shrug. "I prefer French."

My French was good enough to have gotten me this far in the conversation, but I knew I wouldn't be able to hold my own in a probing interview on serious matters. Besides, I wanted to be able to sell the tape for radio.

"Thank you very much," I said, packing up my tape recorder. "We must have the interview in English."

Without further argument, I bid Papa Doc "adieu."

Luckily, back at the hotel, we got a call from Miami, where, several weeks earlier, we had pounded the streets looking for jobs. The caller was Elliot "Biggie" Nevins, a strapping bear of a man who was the program director of WIOD radio.

"We need an all-night program," said Biggie. "If you want the job, it's yours."

The only drawback was the salary: $275 a week—for Karl and me together. But it was a broadcasting job, and we needed it. So we said good-bye to the land of Papa Doc Duvalier, packed up two kids, a cat, a dog, and whatever we could carry in our suitcases, and headed for Miami. Painfully, we separated from my mother, who stayed in San Juan with her art gallery, and our newspaperboy, Robbie, who opted to move back in with his parents for a while rather than go stateside with us.

Once in Miami, with no house, no school, and virtually no money, we checked into an inexpensive motel and prepared to launch our assault on the city. Like true gamblers, we were willing to bet everything on our own ability to make it.

We were also willing to throw caution to the wind and live in high style. Being short on cash didn't stop us from living grandly then, and it hasn't since. I'm somebody who insists that style is important in a world where most people don't care. The truth is, style passes for profundity. People are in too much of a hurry to see deep inside your nature; the only thing they pass judgment on is your sense of style.

For me, the epitome of style was Noel Coward. I first saw Coward in Puerto Rico at the Festival Casals, a gala classical music event in honor of the famed cellist. During the intermission I walked through the lobby of the concert hall and spied a pair of men's patent leather pumps. I stared at those pumps, my eyes followed them up, and there—in living black and white—was Noel Coward. My heart leapt.

He looked the way a man ought to look. I still remember it as though he were standing here now. He wore a white dress shirt with a wing collar, a black grosgrain bow tie, and a double-breasted tux with a very large cowl collar. His cuffless pants were perfectly pleated, his hose were black silk, and his mouth held a slender cigarette holder. His thin brownish-gray hair was slicked back. He looked almost like a caricature of himself.

I never even spoke to him. I just stood with my mouth agape, staring in awe. There's nothing more fabulous than living up to an image—and that's exactly what Noel Coward did.

So, taking a cue from Coward, Karl and I set out to live stylishly in Miami. Off the bat I decided to start my kids out on the right foot and get them enrolled in the best private elementary school in town. It turned out that the place to educate your child in Miami was St. Stephen's. It was where many of the city's best families sent their kids.

Without hesitation we boldly went to see the headmistress—though we didn't have a cent. Something must have clicked because that very day the kids were issued uniforms and were in! Later I discovered it was actually quite difficult to get into St. Stephen's. But we must have said the right things because we were welcomed with open arms.

The only sticky moment during our interview was when the headmistress asked for our address.

"Well," I said, with the aplomb of the rich, "we haven't chosen a place yet."

"Oh," she said, "you must meet Emily. I'll make a call for you." With that she called the wife of a top polo player and bank executive, who came over immediately. It seems that Emily was in real estate and only too eager to help. We hit it off instantly.

"What kind of house are you looking for?" she asked.

"Whatever you think would be suitable," I answered. "But there is one thing I must tell you," I confided. "We don't have any funds."

Extraordinary as it may seem, Emily was immediately

sympathetic. "Ohhh, dear!" she exclaimed. "Down on your luck. How dreadful. Let me see what I can do."

Now, if you walked into any real estate agency in Miami and told the broker you needed a house and had no money, the chances are you'd be standing right on the street with your hand out.

But not with Emily. She swung into action. Before we knew it, she managed to line us up as "caretakers" of a perfectly wonderful estate right next door to hers. At some point in the distant future the mansion was scheduled to be torn down to make way for a condominium project. In the meantime, the house needed looking after.

"If I could convince the owners that you're their type, what do you think you could pay?" she asked.

Karl and I came up with a munificent sum of $250, and Emily gave us the nod. Picture it: $250 a month for a four-acre estate on Biscayne Bay with thirteen bedrooms, an Olympic-size swimming pool, and our own dock. But when Emily showed us the house, which was badly in need of a paint job, she was mortified.

"I had no idea this place was not in top shape," she said.

"Emily, I don't think you should let this bother you," I said, eager to close the deal. "It's quite suitable."

"Well, I think you should pay only two hundred and twenty dollars."

"Whatever you say," I said. And the house was ours.

There was only one minor problem: We had no furniture. Karl managed to convince our boss, Biggie, to give us a thousand-dollar advance on our salary, and with the money in hand we headed for what would become my favorite store: Goodwill.

"Where's the manager?" I asked when we walked through the door. "Just follow me," I said authoritatively. "I'm going to walk through the store, and when I point to something, we'll buy it."

The place was wonderful. I immediately pointed to an

orange table, then a fuchsia sofa, and then a chartreuse chair and a yellow ottoman. A half hour later I had picked out a rainbow of furniture—enough to furnish the entire house. And I had done it all for just eight hundred dollars. The manager thought I was nuts.

"Lady, you want all this stuff?"

"Yes, and I want it delivered," I said.

When the truck arrived at the house, the deliveryman was incredulous as I ordered him about the place. "Put the fuchsia sofa in the living room, the green chair in the family room, and the lamps in the bedroom," I commanded.

It worked. Lamps, beds, tables, and chairs all fitted together in a psychedelic hodgepodge of color and fun. It was Miami, after all, and the hippie era to boot. In those days things could work that would look bizarre in another time and another place.

But the furniture wasn't the end of it. We still needed cookware and dishes, so the entire family went back to Goodwill. The stuff was so cheap that for a quarter apiece we each got to pick out our own set of china. We each picked out our favorite cups and saucers, knives, spoons, and dishes. Then we got some extras—enough for eighteen people.

Back at the house, we piled the china on shelves in the big butler's pantry. There were wild patterned plates with big bold flowers, elegant little cups with gold rims, and multicolored stripes on pottery bowls.

With our china in the pantry, our kids in school, our house furnished, and our lives finally in some kind of order, we were ready to entertain.

It was more like a circus. We'd invite lots of friends over for spaghetti and to share in wonderful repartee around the table. Biggie Nevins and his wife, Rose, were usually there, bringing not only a great gift of gab, but also some fabulous dish Rose had whipped up for the occasion.

After the meal was over, Karl would stand up and announce, "I will take care of the dishes. I don't need any help. I'll do *everything.*"

With that, he'd go in the kitchen and get a bucket and hammer and then show up at the dining-room table.

"Are you through with your dinner?" he'd ask a guest.

Then, while the guest watched in astonishment, he'd take the plate, hold it over the bucket, and smash it with the hammer. One by one he'd smash plates, cups, and saucers until the table was cleared.

The advantage, of course, was that he had no dishes to wash. All we had to do to restock the butler's pantry was go back to Goodwill and buy more china. It wasn't worth the time to wash it.

It got to the point where guests would come for dinner and nudge newcomers as the end of the meal approached. "Wait till you see how he does the dishes," they'd whisper.

If our home life was wacky, late-night radio was even more hilarious. In fact, our year at WIOD was the most fun we've ever had on the air. The call letters of the station stood for Wonderful Isle of Dreams, and for us the meaning was more than symbolic. When Karl and I stepped into that studio and the red light went on, we were in another world.

It was a radio world entirely of our own making. For starters we invented a new radio show format, the call-out show. Unlike my present radio show, which is a call-in advice show, we called out to the craziest people imaginable to generate funny segments. At the time there was no law requiring you to tell people that they were on the air. So we didn't. Instead, we would open the phone book and make calls to people all over the country during our 1:00 A.M. to 6:00 A.M. program. It was nighttime madness.

For months I tried to ring up Fidel Castro. It got to be part of our gimmick. Twice a week I'd dial Cuba and try to reach Fidel, while listeners cheered me on. We never did get through, but we had a heck of a lot of fun trying.

Someone who did answer his own phone, though, was the governor of North Dakota. We called him quite a few times, and he never, never got upset. He always made it sound as though he were working all night when we probably woke him up. Ever since then I've had a fondness for North Dakota, although I've never been there.

Then there was the homeless gorilla we tried to buy. I had read in a newspaper about a gorilla that couldn't find a home. We thought it would be nice to pretend to buy the gorilla and give it to the local zoo. On the air the audience heard me calling to find out more about the creature.

"Is it a boy gorilla or a girl gorilla?" I asked.

Karl and I spent several hours of show time bantering about whether we were going to call it Magilla Gorilla or Priscilla Gorilla. Our next problem was how to get the gorilla from wherever it was to Miami. That meant calling Eastern Airlines to book a flight.

"Eastern Airlines, can we help you?" said the ticket agent.

"Yes," I said. "I want to see about getting a seat to Miami."

Meanwhile, Karl was asking me over the air, "Shall we go first class or coach?"

I opted for coach.

"By the way," I said to the Eastern representative, "the seat is for a gorilla."

"I think we have a problem. Let me get my supervisor."

"That's right," I said to the supervisor. "I want a seat for my gorilla. No, Priscilla *can't* go in cargo."

And so it went. The booking on Eastern took a whole week of airtime. We spent hours discussing whether Priscilla should be nude or dressed, hours discussing what she should wear, hours discussing whether or not we should clean her fingernails and shampoo and set her hair so as not to offend the other passengers.

Then, of course, there were the questions about whether Priscilla should be allowed to have a cocktail, what she should eat if offered lunch, and whether we should order her a vegetarian meal.

We finally ended up ordering her a special dinner.

"No, we don't want kosher," I said to the Eastern rep. "We don't want Arabic either. We want bananas. And whatever you do, don't offer her a drink!"

What finally ended the whole thing was the zoo. The zoo officials got wind of our "offer" and called in to say they didn't want a gorilla. They didn't have a gorilla house, and it would cost thousands to build one.

When that routine got stale, I tried ordering room service at Grossinger's in the Catskills. From our studio in Miami I'd call long distance and order breakfast to a room at random every day just before I'd leave the air. Heaven only knows what the people in the rooms thought—not to mention the staff at Grossinger's.

As for the phone bills, our boss, Biggie, always picked up the tab. We may not have been getting much of a salary, but Biggie let us live the high life on the air in a fantasy world of our choosing.

The reason he let us get away with such gimmicks as calling Fidel Castro was simply that it worked. In broadcasting, there's only one guideline that dictates what you do and how you do it: the ratings. If what you do draws an audience, you're a success. If it doesn't, you try something else. To keep our ratings up, we knew we had to give those night owls in Miami a reason to tune in to WIOD. So we let our imaginations run wild and kept the audience off-balance, wondering what we would come up with next.

Karl, of course, was my foil. He was also our enterprising sound effects man. Throughout the night we'd do an air traffic report. At two in the morning he'd get a paper cup and a spoon, and by turning the spoon around the paper cup, he could make the sound of airplane propellers. Needless to say, at that hour of the morning, there wasn't any air traffic, but we turned it into a funny routine that kept us howling.

Occasionally well-known people would even call in. One of our most faithful fans was Jackie Gleason. He had been calling for months before any of us recognized who it was. One night one of our engineers tipped me off, and once we were on a first-name basis, we became fast phone friends.

Jackie loved late-night radio because he loved to talk. He was doing his variety show from Miami, and calling me up was his way of letting his hair down. One night on the air he said, "Hey, Sally, Minnesota Fats is going to be here. Come on over and shoot some pool with us."

It was an offer I couldn't refuse. The essence of the gambler in me took over, and with Karl standing in the wings, I shot a few with Jackie and Minnesota Fats.

But despite the excitement of such adventures and the creative thrill of doing a show with no holds barred, something in my life was way out of kilter. I had become exhausted. The mental and physical strain of doing the show night after night—and doing it for practically nothing—was finally getting to me.

What made it even worse was that we had to leave the kids alone in that big house every night. We couldn't afford help, and so we were forced to leave our two little girls asleep all by themselves, with only our jumbo black poodle and the cat for protection.

As the months wore on, I'd stand in the shower at night and cry, "God, don't make me do this. There isn't enough money to make it worth it. Don't make me do it."

But I felt I had no choice. The job was all we had. So every night Karl and I would kiss the girls good-bye, get in the car, and do the show. We'd be home before they woke up.

One night, though, Allison called on our direct line with terror in her voice.

"There's somebody outside," she whispered.

Karl drove from the studio to our house in seven minutes flat. There were police cars all over the place. Frantically he rushed into the house to see if the kids were all right. He found them huddled behind their locked door. The dog was going nuts, howling like a banshee.

It turned out that what had initially frightened the girls was nothing more than a police car patrolling the neighborhood and checking each house. When the dog heard the police rummaging about, he started barking wildly. He kept on barking so much that the neighbors called the police. That's why there were so many cars around when Karl got home.

I knew then that the situation wasn't safe and that our time in Miami was over.

"Biggie," I said, "I love the show, and I love you. But we need more money. We can't keep doing this."

"I'll see what I can do," said Biggie.

Two weeks later he hadn't called, so I went in to see him again. "Biggie, what did the bosses at Cox Broadcasting say? You know what we're up against. We have two people working for two hundred and seventy-five dollars a week. I can't treat my children this way; I can't leave them alone anymore. I'm scared."

With a sad look in his eyes, he shook his head. "I'm sorry," he said. "I can't do anything."

"Then tonight's show will have to be the last," I said.

We had just enough time before the show to go home, pack our bags, and get the kids ready to leave.

I got on the air, and at 5:00 A.M. I announced, "This is our last show." For the next hour Karl and I took calls from fans who were regular callers, and we said good-bye to each of them. As a parting gift, a Chinese restaurant sent over a free Chinese banquet with egg rolls by the ton.

Then we bundled the kids into the car and headed north.

Under the doormat of the house on Biscayne Bay we left this note: "To Whom It May Concern: Please donate the contents of this house to Goodwill."

CHAPTER FOUR

Chitty Chitty Bang Bang

WE'RE A FAMILY that feeds on fantasy.

No matter what happens in our lives, we instinctively turn the experience into a major motion picture. That's why, when we quit our jobs in Miami, we threw ourselves into this new state of unemployment with great theatricality and gusto.

We left Miami in a beat-up lime green Mercedes with nothing but a case of champagne, some crackers, and a few bottles of Yoo-hoo. Our attitude was "Take the fun and leave the sorrow." Packed in the car were Allison and Andrea, Karl and I. Then there was our poodle, Fame, which was almost the size of a St. Bernard, and Pussy, the cat.

The case of champagne was from a fan named Pat who really had a lot of style. Most fans think I want potholders. I've had more potholders crocheted for me than any woman on the face of the earth. The potholders stayed behind in Miami, but there was no way we were going to leave the champagne. So off it went with us as we hit the road.

The way we pictured it, we weren't simply going on a little drive north to hunt for jobs. "We're going to see the Civil War battlefields," we told the kids. "Isn't this great?"

33

By the time we got to Gettysburg, we had ourselves convinced this was the biggest opportunity of a lifetime.

It didn't matter that along the way we had to sneak the animals into the cheapest motels we could find. Nor did we let it bother us when all our money ran out and we had to sleep in the car. Being homeless was an adventure. "What could be more chic than sleeping in a Mercedes?" we said buoyantly.

Our family's approach to life is a lot like the goings-on in Ian Fleming's book *Chitty Chitty Bang Bang*. Like the wacky inventor Caractacus Pott, immortalized in the movie starring Dick Van Dyke, we've gambled our lives on the value of risk and instability.

Of course, that kind of thinking flies in the face of popular wisdom because almost everyone else in the world is trying to find stability. But I think they've got it all wrong. It's *instability* that breeds character—a lack of certainty that tests your imagination.

Over and over again in our lives, when there was a crisis, we had got in the habit of running away from our problems to something we expected to be more exciting. On one level, the reality was that we had quit our jobs and we had no money. Further, we couldn't stay in our house because we couldn't continue to pay the rent.

But we couldn't tell that to the children, and we weren't even willing to accept the magnitude of the situation ourselves. Instead, we made up an exciting new scenario and then tried to *live* it.

The result was that our kids never knew what "broke" meant. They never knew that broke is hard or awful. They *did* know when I had quit or was fired, but they didn't know the agony and rejection that came along with the experience.

Always, it was Karl—our own irrepressible Caractacus Pott—who pulled me up by my bootstraps and cheered us on.

"Wow!" he'd say. "This is an opportunity to better ourselves. Let's go for it."

Karl comes by his *joie de vivre* naturally. Nothing bothers him. *Nothing.* To him, life is one big celebration. He's been on his own since he was about thirteen. At the time he was living with his parents in Seattle, Washington. But when his father developed lung problems and decided to move to Kansas, Karl struck out on his own in Seattle.

For a year he lived with friends of his family. On weekends he worked at a grocery store to pay the rent, and during the week he went to school. After a while, though, he sensed it was time to leave, so he moved into a boardinghouse run by a woman affectionately called Mama Scappini. There was Karl, a fourteen-year-old boy, in this boardinghouse with a bunch of winos and a few other assorted oddball types.

Every night before dinner Mama Scappini would ask one of the men to go down to the basement to fill the wine jug. Then she'd whisper to Karl, "Come here," and they'd tiptoe down to the basement and spy on the fellow for a few moments. Invariably the man would fill the jug, and then he'd lie under the spigot of the wine barrel and let the wine run into his mouth.

"See that?" Mama Scappini would tell Karl. "That's the only joy these men get in life. I always give them about five minutes down there."

Karl absorbed the hard realities of life at Mama Scappini's. Yet at the same time, like those winos sneaking their drinks, he learned to enjoy every moment for what it was.

For one thing, he didn't waste time hanging his head in self-pity because he had to support himself. Instead, he did all the things other kids did in high school: He played football, he joined the drama club, and at night he set pins in a bowling alley for extra cash.

On weekends he even got a start in his radio career. A

small radio station gave him a job doing a children's program, and eventually he was offered a full-time position after school. The problem was that the station was located a couple of miles out of town, and transportation was dreadful. Ever ingenious, he talked the manager into letting him live at the station.

Karl's "room" was nothing more than a closet where he stuck a cot. For a "closet," he put a pole over the cot to hang his clothes. Since there was no shower, he bathed at friends' houses. He lived like that for about a year, and the situation suited him just fine because it was cheap; it didn't cost him a cent.

Once he graduated, Karl decided to enter the Air Force. Thanks to his radio show, he ended up on the Armed Forces Radio Service, stationed first in Panama and then in Puerto Rico. But Karl never had the deportment or temperament of a serviceman. The real truth was he got through his Air Force enlistment by playing records and badminton. As it happened, badminton was his general's favorite sport, so Karl turned himself into a killer at the game. He managed to get himself in and out of anything by playing endless hours of badminton with the general and the top brass. He's still the only person I've ever met who knows how to play well.

When his Air Force stint came to an end, Karl turned in his shuttlecock and went to Michigan State. After graduation he returned to Puerto Rico, where he got into radio once more. That, of course, is how we met.

From the very moment we laid eyes on each other, we were soul mates. Something clicked between us, and our mutual love for and addiction to broadcasting kept driving us forward.

It was that same crazy addiction that had led us to leave Miami, quitting a job that was going nowhere and looking toward the promise of bigger things up North. Our plan was first to see the Civil War battlefields and then conquer new broadcasting frontiers in New York City. It was the Big Apple or bust.

When we finally hit New York, we discovered that our fantasies had outrun reality, and we were obviously ahead of our time. At least, that was Karl's interpretation of why no radio station in New York jumped at the chance to hire us.

Luckily we heard of a man who had just bought a radio station in Hartford, Connecticut, and he was only too happy to offer us a job. He hired us to do a two-hour noontime broadcast, with Karl as producer and me as interviewer. And he took us on at the incredible salary of twenty thousand dollars a year—nearly 50 percent more than we had been making in Miami!

We should have known something was wrong when we arrived at the shopping mall where the radio station was supposed to be, and nobody would tell us how to find it. For some reason, every time we asked someone directions, he responded with a sneer. Somehow that gave me a very uneasy feeling.

The fact that the station was in a shopping mall didn't strike me as particularly strange. I'd been around broadcasting long enough to know that radio stations have their own idiosyncrasies. Some are so grand they're awesome. The old, established ones often look like the Taj Mahal, with lots of marble, chandeliers, and brass in the lobbies. Others, regardless of how successful they are, are on the back porches of someone's home or over garages.

This one, as I say, happened to be in a small shopping mall. We finally found it nestled between a dry goods store and a W.T. Grant's that had gone out of business. But the really unusual thing about the station was that there were bullet holes in the window. I began to get this funny feeling in the pit of my stomach, and the lady inside, who had worked at the station for years, confirmed my fears.

"Yes, this station is the most unpopular in town," she acknowledged.

It seems that in the middle of this old Yankee town the previous owner had had nothing but archliberals on the air—and people had actually wanted to kill him!

"Is that why there are bullet holes?" I asked incredulously.

She just shrugged, so I pushed on. "I'm thrilled about the salary," I said, "but if they're going to shoot me, that's it."

Karl, with his usual enthusiasm, turned things to the positive. "Well, Sally," he said casually, "you can duck. Just do the show low."

That's the way it went. With Karl's positive reinforcement, I finally geared myself up to do the noon interview show, all the time wondering where the next bullet would come from.

At the outset I did try one ploy to change the image of the station. "If all the people in this town hate you," I told the owner of the station, "why not stage a funeral and bury the station? You can put all the tapes in a coffin and carry them through the center of town. Then go off the air for two days and come back on with a birth and a baptism. At the very least, it will make news."

He didn't buy it. But for the time being, at least, I had a job. With the thought of a soon-to-be-bulging bank account, we managed to rent a wonderful house on a tobacco field in rural Glastonbury, Connecticut. Since we had no money for furniture—not even enough for Goodwill—we all lived in the family room, where we slept in sleeping bags and ate off the floor.

Unfortunately there never was going to be any money for furniture. Once again I got fired. The salary my boss had so generously offered was really too much for a small radio station like his to sustain. He was new at the broadcasting business and didn't realize that in those days you didn't pay anyone twenty thousand dollars to do a two-hour radio show. As for us, we were too giddy with joy over our supposed windfall to realize that it was barely more than a pipe dream.

Once again we were stuck with a house and no furniture or money. Karl tried drumming up radio jobs for me, but to no avail. One station in Bridgeport kept promising me a job; but week after week went by, and it never came through. In one six-week period we made more than a hundred phone calls to the station, and all we ever heard in response was "Maybe. We'll have an opening soon."

While we waited for my big break in Bridgeport, Karl managed to land himself a job as a waiter in an Italian restaurant. It was the only thing he could think of to do so we could eat.

There was only one problem: Karl had never been a waiter, and he knew absolutely nothing about working in a restaurant. Still, he brought his own unique approach to the job.

To Karl, memorizing the price of items on the menu was just too much trouble, so he did the next best thing: He decided to charge customers according to what he thought they could afford. Somebody who was wearing shabby clothes and looked hungry got a bill for a few dollars. A person who looked as if she were in the chips got a much bigger bill.

Using this technique, Karl managed to hold on for about six weeks before he was discovered. There was nothing more thrilling than to see him come through the door every night with his pockets bulging with change from his tips. The money was all in quarters and dimes, and we'd stack it all up in piles on the table and live on it for the next day. Then he'd go back to work and come home with another day's tips to tide us over.

But it didn't last. It's one thing to be a waiter. It's another to be a Norwegian philanthropist playing free and loose with the owner's money in an Italian restaurant.

Also, Karl had no feeling for things Italian, and no matter how hard he tried, he just couldn't pronounce all those words correctly. With his lack of experience and his unusual approach to the customer's bills, the inevitable occurred: He was fired, and once again we were flat broke.

Then things got more difficult. It began to turn cold, and we didn't have any of the right clothes. The children had never lived in a cold climate, and all of us had forgotten how dreadfully bitter it can get in New England. The situation was beginning to get serious—almost as serious as the dead body in the Dominican Republic. Christmas was coming, it was getting very, very cold, and we had no prospect of a job.

So we did the sort of thing we always do when things look glum. This time we threw ourselves into the role of New Englanders and made fruitcakes. That year everyone on our Christmas list got a fruitcake. If we had had an inkling of how expensive all the ingredients were, we might have opted for something else. But we were in Connecticut, and in Connecticut at Christmas why not make fruitcakes?

Despite all the hustle and bustle of baking and wrapping, the truth was we had a small, pitiful Christmas. The only bright spot was the visit of a young friend from Puerto Rico.

"What can I do for you?" he asked on the phone.

"Bring Christmas lights," we said.

To celebrate, we put up the lights, chopped down our own tree, and ate fruitcake. By now, though, our spirits were headed down toward the cellar. We had lost all hope of the Bridgeport job's ever coming through, and we knew there was only one place to go: warm, sunny San Juan.

On a snowy New Year's Eve we piled in the car and headed for Kennedy Airport. As much as we loved New England, the place obviously didn't like us. We were going home to a place where I would be welcomed back with open arms. My mother was still living in an apartment in San Juan, and it was the only spot in the world where we would have a roof over our heads. Not only that, but in Puerto Rico I had been a star. I was certain that my name was still golden and that I could always get another broadcasting job there.

I was wrong.

No matter how popular I had been, I was no longer wanted. Neither of the two English-language stations had a slot for me, and it looked as if none would open up.

I was learning early what everyone in broadcasting—and in show business, for that matter—finds out soon enough. You can be very, very famous and you still may not be able to get a job. That's the dark side of the industry.

For all the glamour of the business, insecurity constantly lurks just off camera. There are dozens of actors and actresses out there who have been in hit movies or Broadway plays yet who have become absolutely unemployable from that moment on. It has nothing to do with typecasting or talent. It has everything to do with luck.

During the next year our lives came unglued. Karl and I left the kids in Puerto Rico with my mother for months at a time and bounced between New York and Florida, looking for radio jobs. Finally Karl struck gold in Fort Lauderdale with a new twist on selling radio ad space. Billing ourselves as radio producers, we pounded the pavement along an avenue of chic shops and got commitments for advertising spots.

In three days we had collected enough tentative contracts to walk into WAVS in Fort Lauderdale and say, "You don't know us, but we've got pledges for dozens of ads. Just give us a show, and we'll bring you the revenues."

Karl's ingenuity sealed the deal. He knew that for many stations across the United States, the first key to being on the air, even before the ratings, is sales. If your show attracts advertisers, you earn your keep and keep your time slot.

Thanks to Karl, my personal promoter, supporter, and positive thinker, I had another foothold in Florida with a noontime celebrity interview show.

And this time I was ready to soar.

CHAPTER FIVE

Born to Broadcast

EVER SINCE I was a little girl, I wanted to be on radio. In my fantasies I was a voice on the airwaves, who, like my heroes, Arthur Godfrey and Jean Shepherd, could hold listeners spellbound with the power of words.

At night under the covers I'd listen to Jean Shepherd weave his magical tales. He was the only disc jockey turned philosopher on the air. Jean could weave a story out of absolutely nothing and hold you fascinated. He could talk about going out for ice cream and make it the greatest story you ever heard. I was thrilled and enthralled by everything he said, and I hung on every word.

After school I listened to the radio constantly, absorbing the style, the syntax, and the substance of various radio personalities. I yearned to speak with the ease of Arthur Godfrey, whose comfortable voice just oozed naturalness.

Nobody ever told me, "This man has talent." To me, other announcers sounded formal, baronial, "on." Instinctively I just knew it was important to be real, so I listened and learned from Godfrey. I'd sit in my room, with my stuffed animals as my interview subjects, and mimic Godfrey's every line. If he asked a question, I'd ask a question. If he launched into an ad spot, I'd launch into an ad spot. If he paused, I paused.

When his show was over, I'd click off the radio and go into my Arthur Godfrey act for my mute menagerie. I have almost total recall, and even at the age of seven I could repeat Godfrey's entire show from memory—pauses, pacing—everything.

Over the years this fantasy training paid off. From Godfrey I learned how to speak in simple declarative sentences. I also learned the art of timing, pacing, and pausing. I may not have learned how to play the ukulele or to sing, but I tried to integrate a lot he had to offer.

Nothing on radio escaped my eager ears: *The Lone Ranger,* with the sound of Silver's hoofbeats riding off into the distance; *I Love a Mystery,* with the eerie bellowing of the fog machines. The noises, the voices, and the mental pictures they conjured up drew me close to the unseen world of radio. I knew that somehow, someday, I wanted to be part of that wonderfully creative medium.

No matter how pervasive and omnipresent television is, the picture will always be better on radio. Unfortunately, though, in recent years radio sold out its own birthright for a mess of pottage and turned itself into a one-faceted jukebox. Pretty much gone is any imagination or creativity or soul stirring. What's missing is the sound of caring and warmth. What's also gone is the variety. No longer does radio adapt to differences in the people listening, or to regional interests, or to the time of day. The majority of radio stations play rock music, a blaring, disquieting, and uncomfortable sound to an ear that's used to gentler tones.

But when people who were creative and managers who came from the ranks of talent, as opposed to sales, ruled the airwaves, it was wonderfully alive.

When I wasn't listening to the radio, I was reading about it. My room was always piled high with books on the history of radio and the personalities that dominated the field, most of them before my time.

My parents encouraged my obsession by reminiscing

about the programs they had listened to as kids. Back then they had grown up on shows like *Ma Perkins* and *One Man's Family*. Those characters were as alive in our family discussions as TV sitcoms are today. To this day I still don't know which shows I actually heard and which shows people talked about. That's how vividly they were brought alive to me.

Even my grandmother was involved. She was a big fan of Mary Margaret McBride, who was the most successful of all early female broadcasters. My grandmother had once gone to appear on her radio show, and she would tell and retell the story to me in vivid detail. Mary Margaret McBride was so revered that when she celebrated her tenth anniversary on the air, twenty thousand people showed up at the old Madison Square Garden to celebrate with her. Imagine twenty thousand people showing up for an unglamorous grandmother type on the radio. She had the same impact that media and sports stars have today.

I was dazzled by the lure of this life, and I set my sights on a career in the public conscience. I didn't formulate what that meant. I didn't know what I wanted to be. I couldn't spell it out. When you're young, you go for the results. You just want to be a star.

As a child you don't usually understand the sacrifice involved in success and the different paths it takes to get there. If you say to a young person, "You can be a star of sports or rock or television," he'll say, "Fine." He doesn't know there's a difference.

I didn't know whether my future was in theater or broadcasting or the new television. I just knew it was out there somewhere.

My mother, who had pegged me as a communicator early in life, never pushed me. But she never said no either. Instead, she encouraged me all the way. The message that came through to me was: "Do whatever you want, and I'll help you."

My mother was the center of my world, especially because my father was away on business much of the time. I was born in Easton, Pennsylvania, but spent most of my childhood in the comfort and luxury of Scarsdale, New York, with summers in Pennsylvania and long trips to Puerto Rico. My father was a broker who dabbled in everything from rum to real estate.

Pop-up, as I called him, was a large, heavyset man who was known by the older generation in our family as "dashing." He was an immaculate dresser who radiated charm. Maybe I'm so crazy about the work of Noel Coward because, like my father, he was impeccable and classy.

Unfortunately the Noel Coward style is no longer a male image. That has all but disappeared. In today's culture being a well-dressed man is not a priority. Suaveness is not a priority. Elegance is not a priority. Manners are not a priority, and in fact, they're greatly suspect. We've returned to the rough male image. These days rough is much more salable.

Whatever happened to that other image? What happened to the debonair Cary Grant type in *North by Northwest*? Where did those men go, and why have they disappeared? How is it that the hunk on a motorcycle, not the gentleman with the cocktail glass, is the prevailing heartthrob? I don't understand.

Pop-up was one of those gallant gentlemen who treated everyone in the world as equal. If he went on a business appointment, he'd show as much interest in and concern for the elevator operator as for the person he was doing business with.

Most of all, Pop-up was a man who exuded optimism. He had tremendous self-confidence and believed until the day he died that good fortune would always come his way. There was never any doubt in his mind that the next big deal was just around the corner—and that he would always be able to pull it off. In fact, he made enough hits to give us a very good life. But there was a lot of Willy

Loman in Pop-up, a lot of unreality about him. In some ways he was too positive. With him there were no problems—just opportunities.

I say we lived in luxury, but that's because Pop-up told us, "You'll never want for anything." Whatever his true financial worth, he allowed us to believe in a security that probably wasn't there. As a result, like my father, I had an unshakable confidence in myself. To my youthful eyes, the world was my stage and nothing was impossible.

My mother, too, bolstered my self-confidence at every turn. Dede was a stage mother in the correct sense of the term. She had once had an offer herself to be a dancer, but for some reason, she never pursued it. She was very beautiful, a pale, willowy Jean Harlow type with long, flowing blond hair. But her real beauty was the inner kind—a deep wellspring of love, great patience, and encouragement that flowed over to me and my brother, Steven.

Whatever she did, she did it with great panache. She had a quiet sense of theatricality that surfaced in the most unlikely places. When Steven and I were in elementary school in Scarsdale, his third-grade class put on a performance of *Robin Hood and His Merry Men*. Since my brother wasn't too keen on acting, he ended up with a small role as one of the Merry Men.

The curtain went up with Robin Hood onstage, and in wandered about twenty Merry Men. Suddenly it became obvious that no one in the audience was looking at Robin Hood. They were looking at one of the Merry Men—the second one from the left.

It was my brother, and he looked every inch a star. That's because everyone else in the cast, including Robin Hood, was wearing a thrown-together homemade costume. But not my brother. Homemade wasn't good enough for my mother's son. She went to Brooks Costumes in New York City and rented the greatest Robin Hood costume you've ever seen.

He looked so terrific in it that everyone assumed he was

the star of the show. So while the real Robin Hood babbled on with his lines, everyone was waiting for my brother to say something. The audience waited and waited, and finally he had his one line: "How now, Friar Tuck." A burst of applause went up from the audience. My brother was so embarrassed he never wanted to go onstage again.

I think it's important to put in a good word about stage mothers, who as a group have been stereotyped and much maligned. Most of the stories that have been done about them have treated them unfairly. Consider, for example, Brooke Shield's mother, Teri, whom my husband, Karl, has known ever since Brooke was a little girl modeling for the Ford agency in New York. Teri is a phenomenally wonderful woman who has always wanted only the best for her daughter. Despite the bad press she's received for manipulating her daughter's career, she has succeeded in steering Brooke to successful adulthood. As everyone knows, Brooke ended up with both an Ivy League education and a glamorous career—which isn't a bad way for any young woman to start out in life.

From what I know about other mothers of show business kids, most successful stage mothers encourage their children, but not necessarily for their own gain or to improve their own sense of self. Rather, these parents are motivated because they genuinely know that their children are talented.

Without stage mothers, you wouldn't have anybody in classical music, ballet, or show business. Somebody has to tell a child that he's got something special. Schools don't do it, and your friends don't do it, so if your mother doesn't tell you you're special, who will? There's no one else to guide the stars of tomorrow.

That's the way my mother regarded me. When I burped as a baby, she thought it was the greatest burp that God had ever created. She bored friends and relatives with endless descriptions of my every move. When we were alone together, she had unlimited patience. I could prattle on for hours and hours, and she would just sit there fascinated by my tales. Later on, when I ended up in broadcasting, my mother continued to be my biggest fan. She would sit and watch or listen to any show that I would do absolutely in rapture. Among her friends she shamelessly bragged, and she carried pictures and kept a scrapbook of all my comings and goings.

She also believed that it was important for me to expand my horizons, and when I was old enough, she insisted that I learn to play the piano, which I was bad at, and the violin, which I was worse at.

I was a child of infinite lessons: tap dancing, modern dancing, ballet, singing, acting. Today the only thing I could probably do on request is tap-dance—something I've done a few times on my television show—but I have no regrets about anything I did.

It all adds up. I still know about the ballet and about the musical theater. I still read music. All these things help you become an informed and well-rounded person. On television you never know when you'll be expected to move in a certain way or to fill a certain amount of time and space with grace and knowledge. With all my early training, I can do those things instinctively.

Not long ago, for example, I made a guest appearance on the hit TV show *The Equalizer*, playing the part of a talk show host. The talk show role was easy. The hitch was that my character had to make a quick exit because there was a shooting. In a strange way, every dancing lesson I ever had paid off as I made my exit naturally without falling on my face.

Today you find many people going into the theater and broadcasting who have never taken a lesson in anything. Sometimes that works. If you're a natural, you've got it. But every talented person would be helped by being trained.

Some might say I was being groomed to be special. But

my mother's philosophy was that it was important to take advantage of opportunities. If school ends at three, you don't just hang around the house. You take your piano lesson Monday and Wednesday, and your ballet lesson Tuesday and Thursday, and your tap and voice lessons on Friday. On Saturday you go into the city to see a matinee or hear a concert.

With Dede, I saw the Lunts on Broadway, and as a very young girl I fell in love with Julie Harris in Carson McCullers's *The Member of the Wedding*. We went to the theater and concerts constantly.

As for schoolwork, I was never a good student. In fact, I wasn't even special enough to be last in the class. I was always third or fourth up from the last—a real embarrassment. I never got A's, and I don't even remember many B's. I think I was in the C and D category for most of my education.

My parents never once reprimanded me or insisted that I get good marks. Instead of upbraiding me for my weaknesses, they encouraged my strengths. They'd say, "Who cares about that? Does anyone else in your class know how to recite Shakespeare the way you do?"

They could see I had a bent for entertainment, so they lauded and applauded every creative step I took in that direction.

I'm convinced that their approach should be a model for all parents to follow. The way I see it, every child should, to the best of his ability, be given a unique selling point. He should be encouraged to be an authority on something he's good at. If your child is interested in coin collecting, for example, help him become an authority on the subject. If he's the best skateboarder around, give him the freedom and the equipment to get even better.

That's what my parents did for me. They zeroed in on what it was that made me feel special about myself and then let me run with it. I often say that the most important thing to accomplish as a parent is to make your children feel good about themselves. If they do, they can accomplish everything. If they don't, it doesn't matter what they accomplish.

Never once did Dede ask me to earn any money from any of my theatrical exploits. A real honest-to-goodness stage mother might have gotten an agent and dressed me up cute and taken me for rounds of auditions. But she never did those kinds of things. She simply provided me with opportunities for learning and quietly encouraged. There was never any exploitation.

There was only one time I can remember her setting me up for a job. We had heard that there was going to be an NBC radio show about children and literature coming out of 30 Rockefeller Plaza. I don't know whether it was the literature or the lure of Rockefeller Plaza that drew her to the show; but she sent in my application, and I was chosen for the children's panel. That was my very first "professional" job on radio, and I appeared on the show for an entire winter.

At the age of twelve I decided that what I needed was experience in the theater. So I spent my summer in acting camp in Vermont with the MacArthur Summer Theater. The director was Philip Burton, the adoptive father of actor Richard Burton. Richard spent a good deal of the summer at camp with us, and what I remember most about him was his voice—a rich, sonorous voice with a Welsh accent that helped him weave a colorful verbal tapestry.

The MacArthur Summer Theater company was special in another way. It was a traveling troupe, and we roamed the New England countryside by bus and truck, hitting a different town every night with our productions. In a way, it was a throwback to the earlier days of the theater, when people like Minnie Pearl sent out teams of young people to organize theatrical productions in little towns across the South.

I felt like I was in the middle of a Judy Garland-Mickey

Rooney movie, saying, "Let's put on a show." All summer long we lived that kind of fantasy existence, performing in the esoteric Czech play *The Insect Comedy*. It was a heady experience for a young girl, and I soaked it all up, relishing the opportunity to act and be around the sights and smells of the theater.

By the time I was thirteen I had my first job as a radio host on *The Junior High News*, on WFAS in White Plains, New York. The way I got my foot in the door at WFAS was to hang around the station on Saturday mornings, getting coffee for the deejay and putting records back in the record rack. Little by little I was given bigger responsibilities.

First the deejay let me pull the records for him. Later he let me pull the "carts." These were pretaped interviews and advertisements on special cartridges that were arranged on racks in the station. Typically the deejay would arrive late and run around the station, frantically pulling his carts just as he was opening his show.

"A good morning to you," he'd say. "We're starting off with Elvis this morning." Then he'd play the record and run to the cartridge racks to grab his commercials and other fillers. That's when I came in handy.

Every now and then, if he had to go to the bathroom in the middle of his show, he'd hand me a script and let me say something on the air. "It's ten A.M.," I'd announce, "and you're listening to WFAS."

An equally thrilling moment was going "live" on location at the local used-car dealer or high school football field. That's the way local "coffeepot" stations, which was what WFAS was in those days, pulled in the listeners. Local involvement was always a big draw.

"We're bringing you our programming all day from Johnny's Resale Chevrolet," the announcer would say. I'd be alongside him, holding the cords for the mike and watching every move he made, oblivious of the fact that we were standing in some dumpy used-car lot. To me the whole scene was dazzling. It was as though I had joined the circus and been transported into another world.

With that hands-on experience, it was only a small leap for me to tackle my own show, *The Junior High News.* I got to run around interviewing people. Then I went on the air to report what was going on at all the junior highs in the area.

That was really the beginning of my radio career. All those years I had spent listening to Jean Shepherd and Arthur Godfrey were finally paying off. But now it was *my* voice that was coming over the air, *my* stories that held the power to touch people's lives. In my junior high mind, I believed that the whole world could hear the sound of my voice. And I began to feel those first gut-level urgings that this is what I *had* to do with my life.

That's when the monkey climbed on my back. Radio is a disease—an addiction that can't be easily cured. Once you're hooked, it's impossible to be anything else. That's why I've spent my life reaching for the next broadcasting job. Like ski bums and surfers, radio people are an itinerant lot. They spend their lives going from town to town, trying to find their next broadcasting job or hoping to move up to a better market. Or they're trying to get out of the business because the pay's so bad. But the truth is, most radio people can never really leave. Try as they may, they usually end up back at some radio station because they *can't* do anything else as exciting. The monkey is still on their back.

Over the next few years I continued to feed my hunger for broadcasting and the theater in all its forms. I started taking Saturday drama classes in New York City at the Neighborhood Playhouse School of the Theatre, the creative birthplace of such stars as Robert Duvall, Gregory Peck, James Broderick, and Joanne Woodward. In the summers I apprenticed at the Westport Playhouse in Connecticut, doing everything from painting sets to driving actors around.

That's where I met John Forsythe, who had the lead in the play *The Front Page*. Years later we renewed our acquaintance at a telethon in St. Louis. When I pulled out a picture from those Westport days, he pulled out a pen and signed it for me.

At Westport I also appeared in a play with Geraldine Page. It was called *The Empress*, and I had to dye my hair black for the role. The only problem was that when my blond roots started to grow in, the stage lights gave me a surreal appearance: to the audience, I looked completely bald.

It was only natural that after high school I would head for Carnegie-Mellon University in Pittsburgh, which was renowned for its drama department. This was the kind of academics I could tolerate; all you had to do was build scenery and study lines, and I loved it. To be accepted into the program, you had to do a professional audition. Entrance was based not on your high school academic record but on your ability to do a serious monologue, a comic monologue, and a role in a small play. For my serious piece I did Shakespeare, one of Portia's scenes from *Julius Caesar*. That's what got me into college. I probably wouldn't have made it if anyone were looking at grades.

Once I got my foot in the door, there were two things working against me at Carnegie-Mellon. First of all, I was not a very good Method actor. At the time every acting school across the country was heavily dominated by the Method, which meant you *felt* what you were doing as opposed to doing it technically. This approach had been popularized by Konstantin Stanislavsky in his book *An Actor Prepares* and by Richard Boleslavsky in a book called *Acting*. Their theories were being put into practice by Elia Kazan and Lee Strasberg at the Actors Studio in New York. But I didn't fit into the new mold. I was a good actor, but I was a technical actor. I was too "trained."

My second problem at school was that I had itchy feet. I had to be on the go. No matter how hard I tried, I couldn't put up with the 7:30 P.M. curfew in my dormitory, the Margaret Morrison Dorm for Women.

At home my parents had given my brother and me a tremendous amount of freedom. We never had a specific bedtime. We were never told, "Don't bring a lot of friends over." There were no rules—ever—in our household. Curfews and household discipline were completely beyond my frame of reference. As a result, we never wandered out at night—probably because we had so many other opportunities during the day that we were too tired to go out!

But at college I chafed under the restraints. There was no way I was going to stay in a dorm after 7:30 P.M. just because someone said so.

I sneaked out through the garage three times, and each time I was caught. Even the threat of expulsion couldn't slow me down. If you earned three or four demerits, you were kicked out of school, and I was building up those demerits very rapidly. It wasn't as though I were doing anything bad on my forays outside the dorm. I wasn't running out to be with a guy or go to a bar or do anything interesting. I just didn't want to be cooped up.

What finally did me in at Carnegie-Mellon was having to choose between directing and acting. The teachers were steering me toward the directing department, which I perceived as a nice way of saying I wasn't good enough to be their kind of actress. They did determine that I had the type of analytical mind that would make a good director; when I looked at a play, I was able to grasp the total picture.

Later those analytical tools helped me in television. You have to be a good director to be a talk show host because on the air you have to be aware of the total production. You have to know how to pace a show and when to show emotion. Whether you're telling other people how to respond or doing it yourself, it's a directional talent. I'm quite sure that if Phil, Geraldo, Oprah, or I needed another job, almost all of us could direct in the theater.

But back in college I rebelled against directing. In my mind the status was not in being a director but only in being on stage. I saw the writing on the wall and headed for New York, where a new department in broadcasting had just been started by Columbia University in conjunction with NBC.

The classes were held in broadcasting's holy of holies, the NBC studios at 30 Rockefeller Plaza. When I stepped into the lobby, surrounded by Diego Rivera murals and marble, I knew that I had arrived. The echoes of all the great NBC personalities —George Burns, Fred Allen, Jack Benny—reverberated through the hallways. The history of broadcasting was right there on those walls. I just knew I wanted to be part of that.

What was even more exciting was coming face-to-face with some of the great broadcasters of the fifties, who were teaching the Columbia courses. John Cameron Swayze taught me news, and Patrick Kelly instructed me in announcing.

I was sure that with this grounding from the greats, my career in broadcasting would be set for the rest of my life. Getting a job would be easy. I'd flash my weighty credentials, rip and read the news in my well-modulated radio voice, and be an automatic shoo-in for any slot I wanted.

As usual I was wrong.

The last words I heard from the Columbia dean in charge of my program was: "You've got the finest female voice I ever heard, and you read copy like no one else. But you might as well get a job as a secretary."

Suddenly it dawned on me that I was one of only two women in the broadcasting program and the only one to my knowledge who had an authorized major in broadcasting. My degree from Columbia is a Bachelor of Fine Arts with a major in broadcasting, but since the university discontinued the program after two years, I don't think there's another female who has the degree. That should have told me something about the obstacles I had ahead of me.

The top male students were immediately taken on in some form at NBC. Some were hired as pages, and others were put into training programs. But even though I was at the top academically—for the first time in my life, I might add—I wasn't offered any kind of job by NBC.

Women, it seemed, had become *personae non gratae* on the air. Memories of Mary Margaret McBride had faded all too quickly. The prevailing wisdom among broadcast executives was that the housewives of the fifties wanted to listen to men, not women, giving them advice as they did the ironing and cleaned the toilet bowl in the morning. The powers that be reasoned that all women were in competition for men, and every woman hated every other woman. Therefore, women on the air would be a threat to the women at home. Only by listening to the *male* voice could they get satisfaction.

That's what the dean was trying to imply when he suggested that I get a secretarial job. But I didn't listen to his admonitions. Instead, I latched on to the positive things he said about my abilities and vowed to do whatever I could to make my mark. I'd show them!

There were other reasons, though, for my single-mindedness. If broadcasting had become an addiction, in some ways it had also become an escape. That's because my home life had become tragically unstable, and the security that I had come to believe was my birthright had been pulled out from under me.

It all started several years earlier, when my father was stricken with heart disease. I don't even remember when it happened or exactly how old I was, but gradually I became aware that he was in very bad shape. He had a series of heart attacks, which left him unable to work. He kept trying to pull himself together, and every now and then he'd manage some small business deal; but eventually he got to the point where he couldn't work at all. All he had left were his dreams. Day after day he kept telling us tales of a bright future which, for him, would never come true.

We might have scraped by if he had just had insurance. But he had either never subscribed or failed to make payments, because there wasn't any insurance money left to get us by.

I felt betrayed. We'd been promised a rose garden, but in truth, there was no solid financial backing to our lives. All the things Pop-up had promised us were gone.

What I do remember is a series of painful images. While I was still relatively young, in my early teens, we had to move out of our beautiful house in Scarsdale and get an inexpensive apartment in Riverdale.

I can remember standing out on our front lawn, ashamed of what the neighbors would see, watching the movers take away my bedroom set to be auctioned. It was a wonderful set—pine, with a dressing table with little skirted doors that opened up, and a magnificent bed with carved pineapples on the bedposts. I thought it would always be mine. With tears in my eyes, I watched my childhood bed being loaded onto the moving truck. I didn't understand that it was just a piece of furniture. It was part of me. The truck was taking everything I had away from me.

To this day, whenever I see people loading furniture on a moving van, all those memories come flooding back. That image has come to represent many feelings of running and hiding that still haunt me.

Then Pop-up was told he needed an operation. More and more the burden fell to me to make the decisions. But I was too young and unprepared.

"Look, young lady," the doctor said ominously, "your mother's not financially astute, and your father's sick. Do you want him to live or die?"

"I want him to live," I said numbly.

"Then this operation is going to cost about forty-five thousand dollars," said the doctor. "I suggest it's in your hands whether he's going to live or die."

Whether it was in my hands or not, I felt I was responsible. There was no one else. I knew Mother couldn't handle the details of life by herself. She coped best when she was taken care of. Whenever I asked her whether Dad had any bank accounts left or property, her response was to brush it off. "Don't worry your head," she'd say.

Pop-up went ahead and had the operation that the doctor insisted he needed. Then he had another. But neither of them helped. In fact, we found out two years later that the first expensive operation was the worst thing we could have done. Not only was it all in vain, but it worsened his condition. Since then, I've feared the tyranny of doctors and the medical profession.

All the operations did was leave us broke, and broken. I remember people starting to call the apartment and saying, "I want to speak to your dad. He owes me money."

I was young enough, and scared enough, to let myself be frightened by this perpetual bombardment of phone calls. Day after day the phone would ring, and strange people would declare, "You owe us, you owe us."

As the months dragged into years, I tried, along with my brother, to protect our parents from the vultures that were preying on us. When things got too hot, we'd pack up the family and move to another apartment. We even went so far as to change our family's identity to escape the people who were after Pop-up and Dede. For years Steve and I managed to cover the family's trail, and to this day we still keep our family's identity hidden.

In fact, I've buried the truth so well that in my mind my teenage years have become a blur of time and events. The only memories I choose to recall involve the pursuit of my dreams in the theater and in broadcasting. Those dreams, and an early marriage, forced me to run away from the ordeal the family was facing.

Eventually my proud father came to a very ignominious end. He died destitute in a Veterans Administration hospital. By then I was a young wife living in Puerto Rico with no money to contribute to his medical bills. Dede was living nearby in a world of her own. It fell to Steve, who was in the Air Force at the time, to look after Pop-up during his last couple of years.

When Pop-up died, I flew alone to the mainland from Puerto Rico for the funeral. An uncle paid for the burial, but I couldn't bring myself to go to the cemetery. Instead, I just turned around and went back to the airport.

It was all over and done in one day. I flew to New York and returned within eight hours. I remember on the airplane back to San Juan there was a group of businessmen coming from a convention, and people were laughing and drinking a lot. I wished so much that they would be quiet. And I wished I had had enough money to have paid for his funeral—the final debt.

When I got back home, I told my mother about the day. But she didn't want to listen. Or perhaps she couldn't really hear. Like me, in her pain she had blocked it out.

To this day I don't even know where Pop-up's grave is, and I doubt if there's even a headstone. It's too painful to find out. My brother and I, who are very close and see each other often, still never talk about it. It hangs there unspoken.

Maybe it doesn't really matter. Engraved on my heart is the real legacy my father left me: an unswerving belief in myself and a little voice inside me that says all things are possible and the next big deal is just around the corner.

It was that same little voice that was beckoning to me again as Karl, the kids, and I moved back to Miami for still another shot at broadcasting.

CHAPTER SIX

Madcap in Miami

IF THERE WAS ANY one period in our lives when we turned instability into an art form, it was our second stint in Miami. In 1971 we got ourselves a nice little rented house in Coconut Grove and settled in for several years of operating on the cutting edge—some would say on the edge—of balanced behavior.

During those years we established a life-style that has remained unaltered to this day. We lived by the four C's: children, career, camaraderie, and credit. Always on the brink of financial chaos, we flung open the doors of our lives to embrace a wide circle of friends and experiences. Then, as now, we freely cast our bread upon the waters and didn't bother waiting for it to come back.

Our lives were dominated by the need to work. With us, broadcasting is an obsession. It was also a meal ticket. So we plunged into my noontime radio show with a vengeance, always keeping alert to other possibilities to push my career forward and augment our paycheck. Before long Karl had parlayed my broadcasting experience into an additional radio job, doing interviews on a rock music station.

Then, through a miraculous turn of my wheel of fortune, I was named host of *A.M. Miami,* a ninety-minute local morning television show that followed the CBS *Morning News*. Landing this job was more than just a little break for me. *A.M. Miami* was really big-time stuff in Miami in the early seventies, and it launched me as a local media semistar.

I got my break through my old boss Biggie Nevins, who had tipped Karl off about the show and set up a meeting with the program manager. I did a five-minute audition, and a week later I was given the nod.

It was that easy. Sort of. The real truth is, I was not put on the payroll overnight. Unlike Lana Turner, who got her start in pictures when a well-connected Hollywood editor saw her in a drugstore across from Hollywood High and exclaimed, "How would you like to be in pictures?," I was not simply handed the *A.M. Miami* job on a silver platter. I had to work and wait for it.

In broadcasting, every job has a slow, subtle beginning. It usually involves weeks and weeks of waiting. When you go to somebody for a job, he rarely says no. Instead, he keeps you hanging and says, "Maybe." When you go back several weeks later, he'll say, "Maybe."

That's what keeps 90 percent of talented people out of show business. In their heart of hearts, they say to themselves, "If they really wanted me, they'd grab at the chance to get me." But the only time anyone really grabs at you is *after* you're famous. The rest of the time you have to dog people's heels.

At *A.M. Miami* I was offered the chance to work without pay for a couple of weeks so the station executives could see if they liked the show. "We don't want to arrive at a salary until we've got the features in the can," said the station manager. "Then we'll see whether we think we're going to air them." Miami was a non-union market, so stations could get away with such practices.

If I wanted the job, I had no choice but to work my tail off to prove myself. All the while I was hanging by my fingernails, trying to be brave in the hope that the show would come through.

It did. I was put on the air every morning for ninety minutes, interviewing the famous and not-so-famous. The show was *me.* I had no alter ego to interview some of the guests and give me a breather. The only help I had off the air was one producer, a young woman named Rita Eklund, who did everything. She lined up the guests, made sure they got to the studio on time, briefed them, and had all the props ready. Sometimes we had twenty or twenty-five guests on one show—and together we did it all!

By today's standards, Rita was a phenomenon. To put on my syndicated TV show *Sally Jessy Raphaël,* for example, there are four producers and all sorts of auxiliary staff to help conceive the programs, do research, arrange transportation, and line up the guests. But in Miami, between Rita and me—with a lot of help from Karl—we managed to put on a show. The only way we could get through each day was pray that a certain number of guests would show up every morning.

My day was a madcap marathon. In the morning Karl and I got to the TV station at seven, and by nine I was on the air with *A.M. Miami.* When that was over, we jumped in our rattletrap Volkswagen, which had each fender painted a different color, and rushed to Fort Lauderdale, where I did my noon radio show. Then we raced back to Miami to tape another radio interview, which was aired late at night on the rock station.

But I wasn't the only one shuttling from city to city and from program to program. Inevitably a guest who appeared on my television show in the morning also showed up in Fort Lauderdale at noon for my radio show and later appeared back in Miami for my interview on the rock station. Karl was producing my two radio shows; that meant it was up to him to line up the guests.

As a result, he operated on the theory that if you got your hands on a performer—or any person who would talk to you, for that matter—you kept him for the radio shows! Don't let him out of your sight. We wasted a lot of energy trying not to let anybody escape from the TV show. Often we bodily muscled a guest into our car for the next interview.

That's how we ended up capturing Tony Randall, who played Felix Unger, the wonderfully fastidious photographer on the TV sitcom *The Odd Couple.* I had just finished interviewing Tony on *A.M. Miami* and he was about to walk out the door. But before he could make his escape, I rushed over and grabbed him.

"You're coming with us now, Mr. Randall," I said, ushering him out the door. After months of experience Karl and I had learned that performers never knew where they were going next. They relied on someone else, usually a press agent, to tell them what to do. If we looked authoritative enough, most of the time we could convince them to come with us.

Tony followed us into the Volkswagen, and we whisked him to the next interview. When that was finished, it was time to go back to Miami for yet another round of questions for the second radio show. This time, however, he started complaining about a button that had come off his jacket. He's very meticulous—just like Felix Unger—and he was more concerned about the button than the interview.

"Just sit here and I'll sew it on," I said, comforting him.

He tried to protest, but I just grabbed the jacket, took out a needle and thread, and started sewing. All the while I was plying him with questions, as the recorder taped our conversation. I managed to take a half hour to sew one button on one jacket. By the time the button was on, the interview was over.

"Thank you very much," I said to the startled Randall. With that he put on his jacket and walked out.

If Tony Randall was surprised by the turn of events, actor Eddie Albert was positively nonplussed by the circumstances surrounding his visit. Eddie had come to Miami to do a one-day blitz for gardening. He was interested in having people grow their own vegetables. It was one of his pet interests and still is.

Usually, top performers like Albert come into a city and spend a day promoting their causes on every possible media outlet: radio, TV, newspapers, and magazines. It just so happened, of course, that I was almost the only game in town in those days. But I'm not sure Eddie ever did figure that out.

He breezed into the TV show, I asked him my questions and said good-bye. From there he rushed off with his press agent to do two or three newspaper interviews. As if those weren't enough, he was scheduled to see me again in Fort Lauderdale. But the relentless appointments were taking their toll, and by the time he showed up at my studio at noon, he was already worn out.

Once again we were introduced. Eddie looked at me quizzically, as if he thought he knew me or had seen me before. Without cluing him in, I asked him the same questions I had covered on *A.M. Miami*. He answered the questions with great enthusiasm, but during the entire interview he had the most puzzled look on his face.

After the show was over, there was no time for chitchat, since Albert had to run off to do a series of magazine interviews. Unlike Tony Randall, whom Karl and I had herded around, Eddie Albert had had his day prearranged for him. Someone of his stature I couldn't drag around myself. I could only get my hands on a certain level of celebrity.

Eddie didn't know it, but he was scheduled to see me again back in Miami on radio. I was ready for him, but he still wasn't ready for me.

"Of course, you remember Sally?" said his agent as he presented Eddie for the interview.

This time Eddie looked at me as if he really did know who I was. But it was also clear he was plumbing his mind to figure out where we had met before. "Who the heck is she?" he seemed to say to himself.

He never asked where we had met, and I never told him. Instead, I launched into the exact same interview for the *third* time that day: the same questions, the same order. And then he left.

But I wasn't finished with Eddie Albert yet. Karl had cooked up a juicy scheme to see how far we could test his credulity.

"Here's his itinerary, Sally," said Karl. "He's going to dinner at the David William Hotel. Why don't we intercept him and do something wonderfully funny?"

With that we raced over to the hotel, where I convinced the management to let me serve Eddie his drink.

Eddie looked up from the table at me in my waitress uniform, and *this* time he said, "Haven't I seen you somewhere before?"

Without skipping a beat, I said, "In show business, Eddie, you do what you have to do." Then I gave him his drink and walked out of his life forever.

There are other stars I interviewed, though, who reappeared years later on *Sally Jessy Raphaël*. Zsa Zsa Gabor has been on my show many times. On her first visit I said, "Hi, Zsa Zsa, nice to see you again." She drew a complete blank.

Since then I've learned to tip off my guests. After all, celebrities do so many of these interview shows that it's hard for them to remember from one show to the next. I've come to realize that someone in my position can't be too sensitive. Many times I will interview guests three or four times, and like Zsa Zsa, they still won't remember who I am. Now I always give people the benefit of the doubt by giving my name first and then telling them where I met them. They say, "Oh, yes," but I know they often don't have the foggiest notion who I am.

I may not have made a big impression on human celebrities in those days, but with animals it was another story.

I'm wild about animals, of course, even wild ones, so I was always willing to interview various animal trainers and their charges. One morning we had a couple of lovely lions on *A.M. Miami* with their trainer. The lions were very comfortable onstage and paced back and forth as if they owned the place. Every now and then they'd walk up to the camera and put their faces right in front of it.

It was all very relaxed and visually interesting, right up until the very end of the show. It was so relaxed, in fact, that the lion trainer seemed to think it was okay for him to go up to the control room, leaving me all alone with the animals as I launched into my closing comments.

"Thank you very much for being here with us," I said, gesturing with both hands.

There must have been something in the way I raised my hands that was a signal to one of the lions. The next thing I knew, he was charging at me at a fast clip. He leaped up, put his paws on my shoulders, and toppled me to the ground.

The cameraman, watching in horror, did what instinct told him to do: He put the camera on hold and ran away, leaving me by myself to fight off the growling beast.

Meanwhile, the credits were rolling, the music was swelling, and I was lying flat on the floor with a lion on top of me, certain that the end had come. The beast's smelly breath was hot on my face, and his saliva was dripping all over me. The only noise on the set was the sound of the lion snarling.

"This is it," I thought. "This is the way you get it. Good-bye, world."

Moments later the trainer rushed down from the control room and screamed for the lion to stop. In an instant the lion had disappeared, and I was left shaking on the set.

My next brush with the animal kingdom was with a chimpanzee. I love chimps and was thrilled to have one on the television show. But when I reached out to hold him, he took a great big bite out of my forearm.

With the blood oozing out of my arm, I took my other hand and instinctively swatted the chimp. His eyes rolled around in his head, and I thought he was a goner. To anyone watching that day, it was animal abuse—pure and simple. It would have been hard at that moment to convince anyone that Karl and I had once spent hours cleaning out kennels in Puerto Rico for the Humane Society.

My bout with the chimp was a prime example of that old adage in television: It's not what happens that counts; it's what the camera sees.

Luckily, most of my interviews were a lot more tame. Over the years in Miami I interviewed hundreds of luminaries, ranging from New York's Mayor John Lindsay to anthropologist Margaret Mead. Here are some of my reviews:

- Mayor John Lindsay is about as sexy as a politician can get. I saw him again recently, and he's *still* sexy.
- Richard Harris is about as sexy as an actor can get, and I interviewed him and John Lindsay on the same day! I let them do the talking, while I "related."
- Warren Beatty, whose theatrical talent is underrated, is in too much of a hurry to be sexy. He tries too hard.
- Ann Miller, the actress and dancer with the fabulous legs, has one of the most self-deprecating and charming senses of humor of anybody in show business.
- Lillian Gish, who was around at the birth of the film industry, autographed a photo for me. It wouldn't have been remarkable except for the fact that the picture was of Lillian and her sister, Doro-

thy, who had been dead for several years. Now *that's* loyalty.

• F. Lee Bailey, the famous trial lawyer, is terribly intimidating, and I'm not easily cowed.

• Tennessee Williams was so otherworldly he reminded me of Blanche in *A Streetcar Named Desire.* He giggled a lot and fidgeted with his fingers. He was willing to talk to me for hours because I wasn't interested in his sex life. I wanted to talk about his plays. He was a great man with no self-esteem.

For me these interviews were an education in life. That's what radio and television have afforded me. Thanks to broadcasting, I've been educated by some of the world's greatest professors—even those with accents.

The American public will not listen for any length of time to anyone who has an accent. The accent we most tolerate is the English accent, which we automatically assume means somebody is a king or queen or rich. Any English accent, even Cockney, goes over in America.

But the American public will *not* listen to a Frenchman or an Italian for any length of time. In those days, I didn't care who I interviewed because I wasn't earning very much and I simply wanted the experience.

What's more, most of the interviews I did for the rock music station—and later for a classical music station—were simply used by the stations to fulfill their public service requirements. Station owners and managers were then under a mandate to devote a certain percentage of their broadcast day to public interest. A station that was making megabucks playing rock music still had to go for its license renewal. Its lawyers would have to make a case in Washington and convince the Federal Communications Commission that it devoted so many hours a week to public service. Mostly it was a joke.

Usually those public service programs were aired at a time of day when the ratings were lowest. That meant very early Sunday morning or in the middle of the night. Those are the "dog" hours in radio. Almost all Sunday is dog. If you're on at eleven Sunday night, that's *major* dog. Four or five in the morning on weekdays is dog. Saturday morning is rated surprisingly high—because young people are at home and listen to rock music. But as the afternoon goes on, it becomes more and more dog. Saturday night is big dog because the broadcast executives think that everybody's out.

In my heart of hearts, I suspect relatively few people heard many of my early radio shows. But I did them anyway, with such people as Philippe Halsman, the French photographer who is famous for his pictures of jumping celebrities. His photos have all the great people in the world jumping.

No one else in Miami might have known who he was, but I booked him, and I talked to him, and I learned all about photography.

Often the expertise I acquired from these interviews brought me unexpected rewards—and headaches. A case in point: I talked with James Beard many times on *A.M. Miami*, and after a while the word got out that I knew something about cooking.

It turned out that Burdines department store was holding a symposium featuring four or five of the world's top chefs. The food impresarios were coming for a weekend of cooking demonstrations and discussions, and Burdines needed someone to take them out on the town for dinner one night. That's when they called me.

"Pick a restaurant, and send me the bill," said the man in charge of the meeting.

But what type of food do you give people who know everything there is to know about food? I decided on Cuban, which was still a novelty outside Miami at the time.

Once I had settled on a restaurant, the next problem was my kids, who were coming along for the feast. Before the dinner I lined up Allison and Andrea in front of me and said firmly, "You are going to eat with the most famous chefs in the world. I want manners that are impeccable."

We had a dress rehearsal and role-played the whole event, starting with which knife, fork, and spoon to use, how to sit, and how to speak when spoken to. The girls were primed for perfection.

Inside the restaurant the scene was anything but mannerly. Right off the bat the chefs spent an enormous amount of time arguing back and forth about what they were going to order.

When the food arrived, they took their forks, leaned over the table, and started tasting from each other's plates. They were snatching food from one plate to another and discarding the food into their glasses. In short, they were behaving the way food scientists ought to behave.

"Let me try that," said Beard, leaning over to grab a bite from one of his colleagues. "That taste goes with this."

My children saw the most appalling manners they have ever seen. And they shot me a condescending look that said, "How little *you* know."

I may not have known much about the behavior of famous chefs, but I did know that broadcasting was one heck of a way to make a living. As for success, it was always an elusive goal. Just when I thought I had made it as a local star in Miami, along came Sally Quinn, a journalist who admitted she had little broadcasting experience. She took over as anchor of the network's CBS *Morning News* and put me in my place. Since my station was a CBS affiliate, I had to swallow my pride and follow "the other" Sally morning after morning. It was of little comfort to me that her broadcast star fell as quickly as it rose. The fact that a good print journalist had a shot at network television, while I had been working my tail off in the hinterlands, seemed very unfair.

The truth is, sports figures are hired as broadcasters and so are Miss Americas, with varying results. Sometimes the medium shows a lack of respect for itself when it comes to borrowing talent from areas other than broadcasting.

Another sobering reflection on fame was a radio interview I conducted in New York with Barbara Walters, who was then a star of the *Today* show. During the interview she started talking wistfully about her future and what she would do "one day if I ever make it."

It stopped me cold. Here I was, talking to Barbara Walters, who I thought was a household word in America, and she's telling me what she's going to do *if* she ever makes it! I wanted to scream, "What do you *mean,* one of these days you're going to make it? I'm here interviewing *you!*"

To me she *had* made it. But to her she was still on the way. In broadcasting, success isn't a goal; it's a state of mind. That's why I learned early in my career never to dwell for too long on the ups and downs of my career. There were always more important things to consider in life—some right at my very doorstep.

The nuclear family may be the center of life to most Americans, but to our way of thinking, nuclear means what it did to Enrico Fermi: an explosion.

As quick as you could say, "Miami," our family extended and expanded to include an unlikely circle of friends and relations. For starters, Dede moved to an apartment nearby, and our "foster son," Robbie, left Puerto Rico to rejoin our family and continue his education. He's still an important part of our lives. Now he's a lawyer in Connecticut with a darling wife and an adorable little daughter.

Before long, others appeared on our doorstep to become semipermanent members of our household. Somehow I'm always getting involved in other people's lives, more often than not quite by accident. People are forever coming to our home and staying—more or less permanently.

One of these long-term guests was a young seventeen-year-old Irishman named Darragh Owens. Karl and I had met Darragh on a trip to Ireland, not long after we moved back to Miami. We were on our way to the Dingle Peninsula, and when we got to Dublin, I decided to look up the only person I knew in Ireland—a man named Peter Owens, who had gone to school with my ex-husband.

I had gotten to know Peter rather unexpectedly. One day, when I was living in Puerto Rico, my first husband said to me, "A very dear friend of mine is coming to visit, and of course, he'll stay."

"Of course, he'll stay" became a phrase I would hear and use for the rest of my life. Nobody could ever stay in a hotel. Visitors always have to stay with us. I guess it was just assumed, and I went along with it.

So into my life walked this very delightful, elfin man who spoke with a very thick Irish accent. Peter was of the old school, and after breakfast I invited him to get up along with my husband and clear the dishes. I wasn't aware that Irishmen sit and talk while women clear the dishes. That approach to life wasn't part of my existence. I was liberated, and so was my husband. And so I repeated, "Peter, here are the dishes. Please put them in the kitchen."

He looked at me in shock, but since he was also very easygoing and wanted to please, he went along with it. "Just stick them in the machine," I said encouragingly.

And he did. He put them all in the oven.

After Peter went back to Ireland, I didn't think very much about him for years. My husband sent him a Christmas card every now and then, but after I got divorced, I lost track.

More than a decade later, in 1972, Karl and I ended up in Dublin, and suddenly I remembered Peter. We rang him up and met, appropriately enough, for breakfast. This time we ate at a hotel, so there were no dishes. Peter brought along his wife, Norah, and their seventeen-year-old son, Darragh, who was an aviation buff.

"What are you doing this summer?" I asked Darragh casually. "We'd love to have you visit."

You can say that anywhere in the world, and the number of people who actually show up are nil. Except for Darragh Owens. When summer rolled around, who should turn up on our doorstep but Darragh, eager for a summer of youthful experience in the tropics.

He got himself a job working in the advertising agency owned by my ex-husband, who by now had gravitated to Miami, too. In his off hours Darragh helped our foster son, Robbie, wage a mayoral campaign for a man who was later indicted for something or other. And when he could, Darragh fed his interest in flying.

I helped him along by setting up a meeting with Mary Gaffney, a stunt pilot whom I had interviewed on *A.M. Miami.* Mary, who was known as the Flying Grandmother, was the aerobatics champion of the world. This little lady—with her gray hair pulled back tightly in a bun—had trained her body to take the force of several Gs. She'd jump into her short, stubby biplane with big wings, known as a Pitts S-2 Special, and do loops and somersaults and other crazy things in the sky.

She even took me up for a ride once. Although I may have been nervous, I flew with her because I'll do anything to face a fear. Flying upside down with Mary Gaffney made me realize that if I could survive that, I could survive any plane ride for the rest of my life.

Young Darragh was thrilled to meet the Flying Grandmother, but Karl and I thought it would be nice to set him up with someone a little more his age. "What are you doing tonight?" we asked him.

"Nothing," he said.

"It's just as well, because we've arranged a date for you."

About eight o'clock that night a gorgeous blonde drove up in a sports car. Darragh was dumbfounded. Her name was Gloriana. She was from Texas, and she treated Darragh to a real Florida experience. They ended up in the Everglades in a big balloon kind of room with films projected on the sides. Latin music was pulsating through the room, and Gloriana taught Darragh to move to the sultry rhythms.

"How long have you known Karl and Sally?" asked Darragh as the night wore on.

"I don't really know them at all," she responded. "I was walking down the corridor at work when this couple stopped me, twirled me around, and said, 'She'll do!' "

By the time Darragh was ready to fly back to Dublin at the end of the summer, his youthful fantasies had been fulfilled: He had flown with the Flying Grandmother, dated the gorgeous Gloriana, and seen from the inside the not-so-glamorous life of a Miami media star. As we said our good-byes, we thought we had done our duty for Ireland and world friendship and wondered if we would ever see this charming young man again.

As it turned out, the Owens family are like leprechauns, who magically appear when you least expect. Eleven years later the Owenses reappeared in our lives, adding a chapter to our relationship. But that's another story.

It wasn't long, though, before we met up with another charming leprechaun—a rather large one at that—who would add magic to our lives in Miami and ever since.

He was Jay Van Vechten, a public relations man whose creativity knows no bounds. That's why we hit it off. Like us, he'll work hard for a good time, and also like us, his tastes are eclectic and excessive. During his career he's done everything from running soup kitchens for the Salvation Army to creating a bicentennial horse race from New York to California, which was won by a mule!

Jay's the kind of guy who's always coming up with grandiose schemes, like the time he actually cleaned up an island in one weekend. A developer he worked for had built a beautiful golf resort on the Caribbean island of Eleuthera. The only problem was that the rest of the island looked a bit like a garbage heap. The road to the resort was lined with ramshackle houses, and debris and junk were littering the streets.

Jay waged a one-man crusade to transform the place. He got the developer to kick in twenty-five thousand dollars, and then he convinced Juan Tripp, then the head of Pan Am, to fly down several hundred gallons of paint donated by Sears, Roebuck. For manpower Jay went into every village and convinced everyone from schoolboys to grandmothers to pitch in.

With the islanders poised and ready for action, Jay led a weekend assault on grime and garbage. Kids cleaned out schools. Journalists painted houses. And workers from the developer's staff hauled away garbage. In two days the entire island was clean and painted. The people were so thrilled they even named a street after him. If you go to Eleuthera today, you may find yourself driving along Van Vechten Drive.

It wasn't long after his Eleuthera coup that we first met Jay, who was rapidly moving up the public relations ladder in Miami. Ironically enough, it was again my first husband who introduced us. The two men were having a business lunch when the subject of Puerto Rico came up.

"Did you know Sally Jessy Raphaël?" asked Jay. "I'm a fan of hers, and I know she spent some time in Puerto Rico."

"She's my ex-wife," said my former husband. "Why don't you give her a call? I think you'll be fast friends."

When Jay's call came through over our speakerphone, Karl and I were standing on desks at the Fort Lauderdale radio station. The speakers were set up in the ceiling, so that was the only way we could hear clearly. I didn't have the foggiest notion why I should talk to this man.

"Who are you and why am I supposed to talk to you?" I asked him.

"Your ex-husband thinks we'll become great friends," said Jay.

At that point Karl piped in, with Jay, of course, listening to our entire conversation over the speakerphone.

"That doesn't make any sense, Sally. You don't spend time with your ex-husband. Why spend time with his friends?"

Reluctantly Karl and I agreed to meet Jay and his wife, Sharon, for dinner at a local restaurant. From the outset I was suspicious that the whole thing was a public relations ploy. The restaurant was one of Jay's clients, and the manager rolled out the red carpet when we walked in.

Jay and Sharon were nice enough. But I was completely bored by the whole get-together, until the waiter brought out the boiling oil for the beef fondue.

Ultimately it was the boiling oil that transformed the evening—and our friendship. I made the mistake of spearing a potato and thrusting it into the pot of oil. The oil shot out of the pot and hit Sharon in the face. She grabbed at her cheek and shrieked in pain. She was so badly burned that Jay had to rush her to the hospital.

Of course, I was mortified. For days I kept in touch, trying to be whatever help I could. Luckily the burn left no scar. But the impact on our relationship was permanent. As a result of all the phone calls back and forth, our friendship deepened. From then on Jay and Sharon became part of our world, and whatever we did, we did together.

At the drop of a hat we'd be off and running on some adventure or other. Typical was the "all-white picnic" we put together. We were members of a group called the Vizcayans, which helped support and restore an elegant

Spanish-style Miami mansion known as Vizcaya. Every year the Vizcayans staged a big picnic as a fundraising event. It was a costume party, and members of the group would go to elaborate lengths to have the best outfit around. For some people the outing was the Miami equivalent of Mardi Gras in New Orleans.

But we were last-minute types. We never quite got it together until the day of the party. Then there would be frantic calls back and forth among Jay, Sharon, Karl, and me, trying to decide on our costumes.

One year the only thing we could come up with that we all had in common was the color white. We put on everything white that we owned: white shoes; white socks; white hats; white gloves; white suits. Then we took a white lace tablecloth and put it over a white bed sheet, bought some white flowers for a centerpiece, and packed our baskets with white food. It was disgusting. We had turnips, potatoes, cauliflower, hard-boiled eggs, and white bread. And of course, all-white plates and white napkins. The only thing black on the table was caviar—in individual little white pots.

When we got to the grounds of Vizcaya, all the tables had been staked out except one. It was all the way at the end of the property under the glare of the spotlight. But as it turned out, the spotlight was a bonus. When the lights came on, our all-white motif stood out even more brilliantly. The judges thought we were wonderful and awarded us first prize!

My mother thought we were wonderful, too. She captured the scene on canvas, and in my living room in Manhattan is a painting of the white picnic. To the untutored eye the picture looks unfinished because the people are all in white. But now you know why.

In the years since our Vizcaya escapade we've all moved on to even bigger adventures. Today Jay runs his own public relations agency out of a snazzy Upper East Side town house in Manhattan. Although Jay and Sharon's marriage didn't survive, our friendship with both of them has lasted through the years.

Back in our Miami days we all were like a bunch of gypsies, roaming from adventure to adventure with our caravan of friends and family trailing along with us. By some magical turn of the gypsy's teacup, we were fated to have still another young man appear in our lives—by an even more stunning surprise.

I was sitting in the TV studio after my show one morning when a call came through from a social worker named Mrs. Brown, whom I had interviewed many times before. The room was very noisy, and I was having a hard time hearing what she said, but I assumed it was about her next appearance on the show.

"Yes, yes," I said, without really focusing on what she was saying.

"Then you'll come down and get the baby?" she asked eagerly.

"What baby?" I said.

"The baby is here; it's arrived!"

My mind was racing, trying to figure out what on earth she was talking about, when I realized that it was *my* baby she was talking about. A living, breathing, real-life baby.

"What did you say?" I said aghast, finally realizing the enormity of what she was saying.

"The baby has arrived," she said cheerfully. "The one you asked for a few years ago."

In that moment I came as close to stage fright as I've ever been in my life. I dropped the phone, my mouth opened, and like the biblical Zacharias, I was struck dumb.

Then I remembered. Several years earlier, the *first* time we were in Miami, working on late-night radio and living in our Goodwill-furnished mansion on Biscayne Bay, Karl and I had applied to Mrs. Brown's agency to adopt a baby.

Karl and I had always wanted to have a child together.

But having a practical streak, we realized it would be difficult for me to go through a pregnancy and still keep working at such a feverish pace. So we did the next best thing. We contacted Mrs. Brown, a dynamic woman who could tug at the heartstrings with her pitches for adoptive children, and put in an application.

For a long time we didn't hear a peep from Mrs. Brown, and in the ensuing years, when we bounced from Connecticut to Puerto Rico and back to Miami, we figured it was all for the best. Every time I'd interview Mrs. Brown on *A.M. Miami*, she never made mention of the fact that I had ever applied for a child. And she certainly didn't say that she was actually still following up on our request, which I had long since forgotten.

But when a little baby boy who looked just like Karl was put up for adoption, she called me immediately.

Karl's reaction was matter-of-fact. "It's fate, Sally," he said. "He's just meant to be with our family."

Dede's response was more emotional. "You've got to be crazy!" she said.

But when I took one look at him at the adoption agency, I knew that Karl was right. We had requested a baby, with no strings attached. What we got was a perfectly healthy blue-eyed blond who looked more like our family than I did.

On the day we brought him home, Dede walked into the house and started chastising us.

"Okay, you didn't listen to me. You went down there and got this baby. Let me take a look at him."

That was it. She took the baby, screamed with delight, and said, "Keep your hands off him." It was love at first sight. From that moment on Dede showed up at our house every day to take care of this adorable son, whom we called J.J. We named him that because every boy's name we liked started with the letter *J* and we couldn't make up our minds which one we liked best. We figured that when he was old enough, he could make up his own mind about what name he wanted.

From the time we brought J.J. home, he's been a gift from God. We never really stopped to analyze what a baby in the house would do to our lives. Overnight he became part of the family and our routine, and we just assumed that was the way it should be. We just plunged into this new event the way we do everything else and carried on. And we've received nothing but blessings and unbelievable joy from that nondecision ever since.

That's not to say that a teenage boy—which is what J.J. is now—isn't a pain in the neck, doesn't have real problems, and shouldn't be traded in immediately. But who would not want a kid like J.J.? He's growing into a fine young man who's outgoing and personable and fun to be with. In fact, a few years ago he spent some time in Dublin with the family of leprechauns—the Owens family—and every time they looked out the window on their sedate little street, there was a gang of teenagers they had never seen before. J.J. had become the Pied Piper of Dublin and turned their front yard into a teen hangout.

Once baby J.J. had settled into our little household in Miami, it was time for us to shake things up. We had some vacation coming, and there's one rule of thumb we always follow: "It's important to play!" So we packed the three kids in our six-year-old Volvo, which had taken the place of our ten-year-old Volkswagen, and struck out for the Green Mountains of Vermont. That was as far from Miami as we could imagine, and like everyone else in South Florida, we just wanted to get out.

We had got as far as Charleston, South Carolina, when our travel plans were suddenly interrupted.

The rain was coming down in sheets, and we had been driving for hours. As we headed along the highway toward Charleston, we were aware only of the sound of the raindrops on the car roof and the bantering of the kids in the back seat.

Karl was at the wheel, and I was busy trying to keep the kids happy, when suddenly, out of the corner of my eye, I saw something coming right at us.

"We're gonna be hit," I screamed. It was too late. A car towing a boat had run a light and hit us broadside, and we were hurled to the side of the road.

I was too dazed to remember everything that happened, but somehow we all ended up outside the car on the shoulder of the road. We were all pretty beat up, but miraculously we were still alive. Two-month-old J.J. was in the best shape. That's because at the moment of impact Allison, who was twelve at the time, had hurled her body over his in an effort to save him.

The next thing I knew, we were in a hospital emergency room. My head felt as if it were split open, and Karl's had a wide gash on the side. Among the five of us there were a lot of broken bones and ribs and things.

But what makes our car crash story different from almost any other you've ever read was the timing of this catastrophe. We have either the world's best timing or the world's worst—you be the judge. It so happened that when our crash occurred the entire city of Charleston was on emergency status. Storms had caused heavy flooding, and there were still flash-flood warnings all over the place.

The hospitals in the city were filled with flood victims. In the emergency room where we found ourselves, beds and bodies seemed to overflow into every available hallway.

As woozy as he was, Karl figured out fast that we were not exactly at the top of the triage list. A nurse had given us a preliminary once-over and told us we'd have to wait. It quickly became clear that there was no way we were going to get special attention, or *any* attention, for hours. All I could think of was the Alfred Hitchcock movie *Lifeboat* about a group of people adrift on the ocean. With the food and water nearly exhausted, it was decided that someone had to be thrown overboard.

From the looks of things in that Charleston hospital, clearly, that was us! The truth was, there was no room at the hospital—for us or anybody. And the last thing I wanted to do was stick around an emergency room with two preadolescent girls and a two-month-old baby.

Karl came up with an ideal solution. "I'll tell you what," he said cheerfully. "Let's spend our vacation here in Charleston!"

We hobbled out of the emergency room, hailed a cab, and headed for the best hotel in town. As usual, we were broke. But we had plastic, our credit cards, which got us into a lovely three-room suite.

In the long run the hotel was a lot better for our health than the hospital would have been. We immediately arranged for a doctor and nurse to make house calls, and then we took turns taking care of each other.

Although I did have a concussion, little by little we got better.

The only problem was that the TV station in Miami got wind of the accident and announced over the air that we all had been killed.

Two days after the accident I called the director, Gary Petty, and said, "Hi, guys!"

"Sally, where are you?" Gary said frantically.

"I'm at a hotel in Charleston, and we're having a wonderful time."

"What are you doing at a hotel? We thought you were dead!"

"Oh, we're all sitting here watching TV and eating a lot."

"Come onnnn," Gary groaned.

What seemed bizarre to everyone else appeared perfectly normal to us. The way we see things, why spend ninety dollars a day in a hospital when you can live like a king in an elegant hotel for seventy-five? To us there was no question about what to do, especially since only one— the hotel—took a credit card.

If you want to survive these days, you may have to think credit card. It's taken awhile for the rest of the world to catch up with us on this score, but I'm afraid everyone finally understands. Even the Catholic Church has given its imprimatur to paying with credit: It now issues a Caritas card, which assures the church of a certain percentage of each purchase.

I can understand this way of thinking perfectly. Karl and I had a religious devotion to credit long before the church did. For at least a decade we couldn't pay our credit cards in full. Every time a crisis came up or an adventure beckoned, I'd say to Karl, "What will we do for money?"

"Get the credit cards out," he'd reply. "Let's see if they work!" Miraculously they always did. They worked especially well for trips abroad—like the Ireland junket that brought us in touch with the Owens family. That was one of many trips that we couldn't afford to take but went on anyway. Somehow, when the bills came due, we always managed to pay the amount that was necessary to maintain our credit. We'd take a trip on our credit card and skimp on something else to pay the bills.

The way I see it, it's all a matter of priorities. Some people like fancy cars and will put themselves in hock to drive around town in flashy vehicles. Others will opt for glamorous clothes. We put what money we have in travel and make do with beat-up Volvos and whatever clothes we happen to have in our closets.

Happily, we made the best of the accident and lived it up on credit in Charleston until we were well enough to go home. With our Volvo out of commission for good, we managed to get a cheap flight to Miami and settle back into our helter-skelter routine, always ready to let more good times roll.

But as gamblers we should have been on our guard. Most gamblers know that bad luck runs in threes, and the car crash should have been a warning that there were more disasters ahead. As it turned out, we *were* in triple trouble. Not long after the crash, disaster struck again—and again.

The call came early one Sunday morning.

I could tell by the way Karl was acting that something was very wrong. I knew it would happen this way. That's why I always had Karl pick up the phone. I've always worried that bad news would come by phone, and now my worst fears were being realized.

His face, usually lively and smiling, was drawn and ashen.

"Your mother has been raped, Sally," he said.

I grabbed the phone and heard the news from Dede herself. She had been asleep, she said, when a young man came through the window, held a knife to her throat, and raped her. The attacks continued for a three-hour period. He had left her in a heap on her bed, bleeding and shaking.

"Please don't tell anyone," she begged, mortified that such a terrible fate could have befallen her. She didn't want to go through the agony and embarrassment of describing the incident to the police. In those days it was all too shameful for an elderly woman of her generation to consider.

We did what Dede said and kept mum. We never called the police, and we never told a soul, except the doctor who examined her afterward. Dede felt there was too much at stake for all of us. I was somewhat of a celebrity in Miami, and something like this would have dragged Mother's name through the papers. She would have become the object of intense scrutiny, and it would have devastated her.

When we got to her apartment, she appeared to be stable. Over the next few days, when she came over to baby-sit for J.J., we didn't notice anything unusual about her behavior. She was a little slower, perhaps, but not enough to cause concern. She never mentioned the incident again, and we assumed she was made of strong stuff and able to cope mentally and physically with the ordeal.

Things seemed to be going so well with her, in fact, that about a month after the incident I figured we all could use some fun. I booked a suite at the Playboy Hotel, which had invited us to visit. Then I invited Jay and Sharon Van Vechten to join Karl, the kids, Dede, and me for a night of luxury.

We couldn't afford room service, so Jay and Karl went to Burger King and came back with bags of hamburgers, which we feasted on in the middle of this lavishly appointed room.

Dede, though, wasn't eating much. She nodded her head to her chest, and we couldn't wake her up. When she came to, she was very disoriented. Her speech was slurred, and she couldn't stand up by herself.

"I think Mother may be drinking too much," I whispered to Karl.

By the next day Dede was dragging her foot when she walked, and we realized her problems were much more serious. She had had a stroke. The rape had finally taken its toll.

Dede never did recover. Little by little her condition worsened. Before long, it was so bad that she could no longer take care of J.J.

Karl quickly learned to do diapers and formula and assumed all the child-care role in the household. To him it wasn't emasculating or "women's work." It was a job that needed to be done for the sake of our son, and he did it, willingly. Meanwhile, I was running from Miami to Fort Lauderdale and back, doing three shows a day and trying to keep the paychecks coming.

As for Dede, there were other strokes, and she gradually deteriorated over the next year to the point where she couldn't care for herself anymore. Reluctantly we had to move her into a nursing home.

But our lives were never the same.

That's when the third disaster struck. It was Thanksgiving Day 1974 and I was blithely basting a turkey on *A.M. Miami* when I looked up and saw the program director, Lee Eden, standing behind the cameraman.

I knew instantly that he wasn't there to eat turkey. A program director does not show up on a holiday to bring good news. In fact, for us it was the worst possible news.

I had been fired.

What hurt the most was that in the weeks and months before, there had never been any hint that I was on the way out. But perhaps I had been blind to the clues.

Over the years the show had changed from its original format. When I had started out, *A.M. Miami* was a fun, newsy show that featured celebrities and local color. It was good, light, morning wake-up fare.

But when the Watergate scandal broke in *The Washington Post*, the fallout from that seemingly remote event hit my TV show. That's because the station that carried my show, WPLG, was owned by Post-Newsweek, and Post-Newsweek was Katharine Graham. For some reason, the lawyers for the TV station believed that Nixon crony Bebe Rebozo would challenge Kay Graham's license in Miami and try to get the station. The only way to counter such a threat, the lawyers reasoned, was to prove that the station was doing such wonderful public-interest programming that the FCC wouldn't dream of rocking Kay Graham's boat.

So I was instructed to kill the "entertainment" and focus on public-service features. Instead of wonderful, fun celebrity pieces, I had to have regular interviews with officials like the water commissioner.

But people will not watch weekly visits with the water commissioner—even though the FCC may be thrilled. All this made for some terribly boring broadcasting. For that matter, I was as bored as anybody! Little by little the ratings slipped, and so did the time allotted for the show. What had begun as an entertaining ninety-minute morning show ended up as a rather dull thirty-minute public-information broadcast.

But no matter who or what was to blame for the show's demise, the consequences were the same. I was out of a job, and I had to tell the family around the Thanksgiving table. What's more, the radio shows weren't enough to keep us going.

Once again we had only one choice: the Big Apple or bust! We had left Miami before, and we could do it again.

But this time around it was a lot harder to pull up roots. Dede, the woman who was dearest in the world to me, was sick and alone in a rundown nursing home, and for the moment there was no way that we could bring her with us. I felt so helpless; so guilty. And I had a desperate need to get her out of there.

What I carried with me on the plane to New York, though, was an overwhelming sense of gratitude for the opportunities she had given me. And I was reminded of an interview I had had not long before with a professional violinist whose father had nurtured him in his career as Dede had done for me.

The violinist had been the fiddler for *Fiddler on the Roof,* and he had come on *A.M. Miami* to perform and talk about his background. After the show was over, I noticed an old man standing off camera in the shadows.

"Is he with you?" I asked the violinist.

"He's my father," the musician said. "I take him with me everywhere I go."

"That's wonderful," I replied, marveling at their closeness.

"You see," said the violinist, "when I was a young boy, I didn't want to practice the violin. But even though I objected, my father made me practice. He knew that I had talent. Now I take him with me as I travel because I owe him a great debt. It isn't just my career. It's *our* career."

That was the way it was with Dede and me, I thought wistfully. Soon, very soon *our* career would take off. Maybe then Dede could be with me in New York.

CHAPTER SEVEN

A Bite of the
Big Apple

A FEW WEEKS before we left Miami for New York, Karl had gone ahead to reconnoiter. He had taken my résumés and tapes to various radio and TV stations, but to no avail.

"She's too relaxed," he heard again and again. "How come she didn't push the cough button?" (The cough button is a little device you can push to cough or blow your nose while you're on the air. That way no one listening knows you're a human being.)

Many producers continue to think you are supposed to be just the "announcer." But what they get is a person with an authoritative delivery who sounds as if she's "on the air." I could never read the news that way and feel comfortable.

Since no station seemed ready for my more relaxed style of broadcasting, our only hope for an income seemed to be the job Karl had landed with the Ford modeling agency, developing a new broadcasting division.

We used the last of our savings as security and rent on an apartment on the now-chic Upper East Side. I don't know how we did it, but we did it. We've been in the same place ever since.

With a roof over our heads, we settled into a life-style that was rare on the Upper East Side but well known to thousands of other New Yorkers: a condition of near poverty. Karl's job at Ford gave us just enough to scrape by. By the time we paid the rent and the modest tuition at the parochial schools the girls attended, there wasn't much money left over for anything else.

This type of poverty can make you down-in-the mouth depressed all the time, or it can be a terrific challenge. I opted for the challenge. The truth of it all is that apart from the fact that I didn't enjoy being unemployed, I absolutely *adored* being dead broke in New York.

For a couple of months in 1975 we even existed on food stamps. There's just something exciting about figuring out how far you can stretch a book of food stamps. You have to be creative. It becomes a giant jigsaw puzzle as you work out your nutritional needs and break them down into enough food to feed a family of five, plus pets.

Since I was out of a real job, I made a career out of comparison shopping at the supermarkets. I'd shop the specials, walking six blocks from one store to the next, hunting for bargains. I would do this all day long, happily pushing J.J. in the stroller. Every store that had a penny off this or a penny off that, I'd hit. We were also in the coupon-collecting category, and we became thrift shop junkies. There were fabulous thrift shops in New York, especially on the Upper East Side. Since I was already a devotee of Goodwill, I knew how to hunt for bargains in a bargain store. I'd wait for the fifty-ninth markdown and walk out with some nifty purchase for just a dollar.

When I wasn't bargain hunting at the grocery store or thrift shops, I was enjoying the city. New York is the greatest free city in the world if you look hard enough. I'd make a study of where the free museums were and of the nights you didn't have to pay at the others. I saw every off-off-Broadway show that you could get into by making a small donation. I frequented the public libraries with their kiddie programs for J.J. I walked, and walked, till my feet ached. But my spirits were higher than the Empire State Building. I was finally in New York City, and I had hope.

Of course, every week I'd also keep trying to sell my way into a radio or TV job. "I'll be a disc jockey," I said, pulling out my disc jockey résumé. When that didn't work, I'd change the résumé. I had a disc jockey résumé, a news résumé, and a television résumé at the ready, in case someone needed me.

No one did.

Meanwhile, Karl was doing his thing at Ford, bringing home wonderful stories about the gorgeous models he saw every day. One of them was Brooke Shields, who was just a little girl at that time.

I never minded hearing about Brooke Shields. She was just a kid. It was those other women who were getting on my nerves. After all, it's one thing for a woman like me who's been making it since she was thirteen years old to be broke and out of work. It's another to have a husband working at the Ford modeling agency. Imagine the problem: I spent the day making ends meet on food stamps, while he was having lunch at a great restaurant with Lauren Hutton.

Typically I'd come in from a long day of grocery shopping, and Karl would announce, "Guess who I had coffee with today? Cristina Ferrare!"

Down went my self-esteem. I realized fast that for anyone to survive this mental torture day after day, you really had to be made of tough stuff. You genuinely had to like yourself—even if you weren't a model. I had the chance to put myself to the test at Eileen Ford's annual Christmas party, when I was juxtaposed to a roomful of the most gorgeous women in the world.

Eileen and her husband, Jerry, are wonderful business people, and they were always very good to us. It was only natural that they would invite me to join Karl for their big holiday bash. Karl suggested that it would be politic for me to show up.

"I can't go, Karl," I insisted. "I've gained fifteen pounds on food stamps, and I have nothing to wear. The thrift shops have already sold out their party dresses.

"Besides, you expect me to walk into a room where there are no ordinary people, only beautiful models and the men whose job it is to photograph them?"

"Yes," he said.

"That's asking a lot," I said. With his assurance that I wouldn't feel out of place, I agreed to go.

"I guess everybody deserves to be the least attractive person on any given day," I said with a laugh. "But why me?"

When I showed up at the party, though, all my fears melted away. As I looked at the faces of the people who were paid to be the most beautiful people on the face of the earth, I discovered that these people weren't gorgeous at all. They were cleverly put together, certainly, and many of them had a lot of panache; but physically none of them was as beautiful as her photographs in the magazines. Every one of them was flawed. Some had flabby thighs; others had stringy hair; others had gaps in their teeth or noses that were slightly off kilter.

Instead of feeling like an outsider, I fit right in! I went home to my food stamps and beat-up furniture, convinced that all was right with the world. It was a great Christmas gift.

Despite the joy that poverty brought into our lives, we did have our down moments. But they never lasted long. That's because Karl always found a way to get me up and out of the house.

"Let's go shopping," he'd say.

Karl is one of that rare breed—the male shopper. In the past men used to have to be secretive about their obsession and shop mainly from catalogs. But now men like Karl can come out in the open. They can be honest about this.

So, with Karl in the lead, we'd all jump in the car and

head for an auction or flea market, where we could indulge in our favorite sport, collecting. To us it never really mattered what we were collecting, so long as we were shopping for something specific.

What do you collect when you're compulsive collectors like us and have no money?

Eggbeaters. They were the cheapest thing we could think of to hunt for. We gave ourselves a two-dollar limit, and usually for a dollar or so we walked away with a wonderful treasure.

As a result, I have what may be the world's greatest collection of eggbeaters. Today they're all stuffed in a box along with my toy train collection, but one of these days I'll clean them off and mount them on the wall properly.

But at the time we amassed these marvelous gadgets, they served their purpose. Without realizing what we were doing, we had discovered a cure-all for the doldrums: shopping therapy. When you've got nothing to do with your time, shopping gets you off your duff, away from the television, and into a world of people and activity. It gives a sense of order to your day, a chance to be creative, and the excitement of finding a much sought-after treasure. I'm convinced that collecting is the answer to America's problems. People don't need psychiatrists. They need to go shopping!

Eggbeaters may have kept our minds off our poverty, but the truth was, we needed more than eggbeaters to survive in New York. We were blissfully unaware of how bad things had gotten until our old pals Jay Van Vechten and Sharon arrived from Miami on their way to Moscow. Traveling with them were our dear friends Paul and Keith, who had worked on my TV show in Miami.

Paul and Keith took one look at the kids' threadbare coats, which I had so proudly purchased at a thrift shop, and marched them straight to Saks Fifth Avenue. There they outfitted Allison, Andrea, and J.J. in the classiest coats they could find. Back at the apartment they gave all the kids haircuts. Then they flew off to Russia, knowing that they had done their part for the poor in America.

The day finally came when I had to give up food stamps to take a part-time job at WINS Radio in New York. I knew I couldn't continue to receive food stamps in good conscience. But I hated to give them up. I had gotten so absorbed by the food stamp routine that I sat in my living room one day weighing the alternatives.

"Should I leave broadcasting and remain on food stamps?" I asked myself.

But as tempted as I was by the prospect of a free lunch, my addiction to radio was more powerful. So I signed on with WINS.

Everyone in broadcasting who's worth anything has probably worked at WINS at one time in his career. That's because WINS was famous for hiring broadcasters as "temps." The station probably saved millions of dollars over the years by not hiring many permanent employees. As a result, it could get experienced people like me, who were desperate for jobs in radio, and hire them for as long as they wanted.

I was hired to be an overnight anchor on the all-news program. Karl had convinced the station to hire me because I satisfied two minority requirements: I was a woman, and my "home" was Puerto Rico.

If I had known what I was in for, I might have stayed on food stamps. The work was incredibly intense. I'd spend a half hour writing my own news copy—which had to be timed exactly to the minute—and then I'd spend the next half hour on the air delivering the news. That's how it went for six solid hours: a half hour of writing and a half hour of announcing. It was a killer.

But that wasn't the worst of it. At 5:00 A.M., after my first night on the lobster shift, I stumbled out onto Park Avenue South just as the dawn was breaking. To my horror, I discovered I wasn't the only one on the corner at that hour of the morning. Lined up next to me was a row of prostitutes waiting for their pimps.

WINS was on the very spot where the pimps picked up the night's earnings from the ladies of the night. As I stood there, trying to hail a cab, cars cruised up and down the street, stopping at each hooker and collecting her cash.

To make matters worse, one of the hookers nearly accosted me. "If you know what's good for you, honey, you'll beat it," she said threateningly.

Night after night, for the entire year I worked at WINS, the scene was the same. Inside the studio I battled the deadlines, and outside I battled the hookers. By the time I dragged myself home I'd scream, "Karl, you've got to *do* something. I can't stand this anymore!"

Ever the supportive husband, Karl would say reassuringly, "You can do it, Sally. You can do it."

Gradually I became so desperate to leave that during the day I walked from station to station with my résumé. It wasn't just the hard work and the hookers that bothered me. There was just something undignified about being a part-time employee, even if the pay was good.

Finally WMCA, then one of New York's top radio stations, gave me the break I needed. Karl had been pleading with the station like crazy. "Please use Sally, please use Sally," and I guess they finally gave in. For starters, they let me fill in for some of their regulars.

My very first job was to stand in for the legendary host Barry Gray. The station had called me with only a few hours' notice.

"Barry's sick. Can you do the show tonight?"

A tingle went down my spine. "Oh, gosh, here's my big chance," I thought.

When I got to the show and realized my first guest would be feminist Bella Abzug, I was sure I had a winning interview on my hands. After all, "Battling Bella" was always good for a story. She made great copy wherever she went, and she was always ready to take on the most obnoxious questioner. Nothing stood in the way of Bella and women's rights, or so I thought.

Bella breezed into the studio, and even I was intimidated. "Mrs. Abzug, I'm so pleased to meet you," I said. "I'm Sally Jessy Raphaël, and I'm filling in for Barry Gray tonight."

"*Filling in?*" she bellowed. "You mean, my friend Barry isn't going to be here?"

"Well, Bella, I've got to make a success of this. This is my big chance. Couldn't you just—"

"Sally," she said, cutting me off, "I really want to come back when Barry's on."

Despite my entreaties, off she went.

Now I was *really* scared. I had spent what little time I had had preparing for an interview with Bella Abzug, and with only moments to go before airtime, she had just disappeared. Without a guest, what was I going to do?

I had no choice but to open the phone lines and just talk to people about whatever was on their minds. It wasn't the greatest evening of broadcasting, but it saved me from further humiliation.

As for Bella, I must confess that for years after that I held a grudge against her. Even though I tried to be understanding about why she had dumped me, I couldn't forgive her. Perhaps she was tired that night and didn't want to deal with a stranger whom she couldn't predict. Or perhaps she had been looking forward to a feisty political debate with Barry and wasn't sure I was up to the task. Whatever her reasons, though, it was a real body blow to be rejected by one of the country's leading feminists when I—another female—desperately needed a break.

But my attitude shifted radically just a couple of years ago, when I learned how important it is in this business never to close a door on anyone. We were planning a TV program on feminism for my show *Sally Jessy Raphaël*, and the producers had lined up several rabidly antifeminist men. It was clear, though, that to make a lively show, they needed somebody to take them on. That's when I remembered Bella.

"If you want a really good show, and if you want a woman who knows her stuff, you've *got* to get Bella Abzug," I blurted out. I nearly choked on my words, but I knew I was right.

Bella came, and she was awesome. She was feisty; she was combative. In short, she was everything I had hoped she would have been more than a decade earlier. What's more, the two of us clicked so well it was as if we had been friends all our lives.

I didn't have the guts to tell her the impact her rejection had had on me at WMCA years before. But it no longer mattered. What did matter is that I had a new acquaintance and a new respect for the way things work in this business. The truth is, time can heal old wounds—in ways you never expect.

Bella or no Bella, my debut on WMCA did not signal the end to my career with the radio station. It turned out to be just the beginning. This time it was another woman, a passionate *non*feminist named Ruth Meyer, who let me in the door.

Ruth was the "bulldog" of radio. She was an incredibly talented station manager, a cantankerous, lovable lady who worked hard for whatever position she achieved. One of her greatest achievements was putting together the "Good Guys," a lineup of disc jockeys and a program format that made WMCA one of the country's most successful radio stations.

Month after month Karl kept badgering Ruth on the mistaken idea that she should hire me because I was a woman.

"I hate women on the air," she would retort.

Finally she agreed to sit down and talk. There was only one problem. After months of working part-time at

WINS, I had just been offered a full-time job by the parent company, Westinghouse. The job wasn't at WINS in New York, though. It was with KDKA in Pittsburgh, and I was scheduled to start work immediately.

I certainly was grateful for the offer. But how could we leave New York? We had an apartment we loved, the kids were settled in school, and we had even survived food stamps to make a go of it in the city. How could we pull up stakes and uproot the family again when it seemed we had only just arrived?

In a last-ditch effort to keep me in the city, Karl begged Ruth to see me on the eve of my departure for Pittsburgh.

She arranged to meet me at one of my favorite rendezvous, a small hotel bar in midtown. For some reason I got the time wrong and arrived an hour early. With nothing else to do, I started chatting with a man at the next table, and when he offered me a bottle of wine, I happily obliged. We were having a wonderful chat, drinking the wine and talking from table to table, when I realized to my chagrin that I had finished the bottle of wine.

What's more, Ruth was an hour late, which meant that by the time she arrived, I had been sitting there drinking for two hours. When she did show up, we ordered more wine, and the two of us talked on into the night.

By the time I got home, I had only the dimmest notion of what we had discussed. I remembered her frowning and saying, "I don't like women on the air." But I also recalled that she had said one or two nice things about me.

In my confusion I fell into bed, expecting to get up and catch an early-morning plane to Pittsburgh for my first day on the job. But at 3:00 A.M. I sat bolt upright in bed and started to shake Karl.

"Karl, I have to tell you something. I just remembered what Ruth told me before I was too drunk to listen. She said, 'You can come to work for us at MCA.' "

"Let's be calm, dear," said Karl. "Let's be calm." But he

immediately picked up the phone to cancel the flight to Pittsburgh.

The next morning I called Ruth to confirm our conversation. "You'll have to forgive me," I said meekly. "But I'm not quite sure I remember what happened last night."

"I hired you!" she said.

"Right. Thank you."

With that casual beginning in 1976, I embarked on five years of talk radio with WMCA. At the time the station was going strong. It was one of the top ten stations in the city, with a lineup of some of the best broadcasters in the business. Steve Powers was the morning man, and I came on from ten to two. Then came Barry Gray, Bob Grant, and Long John Nebel. Even now, as I list their names, I feel overwhelmed, thinking about all that talent and how lucky I was to be among them.

For these men, as with most broadcasters I know, being on radio wasn't just a way to make a living. It was life itself. When you're on the air, you are *alive*. This was never more true for anyone than for Long John Nebel, who had been on WMCA for years.

When I first came to work at WMCA, Long John was in his decline, dying of cancer. In earlier days he had been a "carny man," who had once managed a pair of Siamese twins and hustled "Imported Chinese Corn Remedy" in Times Square. Somehow he had found his way from there into radio. The same "flimflam" talent that served him well on the streets of Times Square made him a natural for the airwaves.

Long John had what his generation of broadcasters, Jean Shepherd among them, was blessed with: the gift of gab. He wasn't Irish, but he was magic. He could sway people simply by the sound of his voice. The only remnants of that style today are the televangelists. But Nebel was an evangelist of another sort. He could talk on and on through the night, on topics sacred and profane, and millions of people believed every word he said.

He even had me fooled. I first bumped into him in an elevator at WMCA, and by the time I arrived at my floor, he had me convinced that some elevators in New York ran sideways.

"Are you aware of the arcade under Rockefeller Center?" he asked. When I nodded yes, he said, "You can go down in the elevator, and then it runs under the street along the arcade."

A few weeks later, when I learned the truth, I said to Karl, "If he can do that to me, no wonder that man is a genius."

He was a genius, but he was dying. At the time I met him, he did an all-night show of interviews and conversation. During the night, when his strength gave out, some of his coterie of regulars would fill in for him. The regulars were a group of eight or so friends who would hang around and talk if the guests didn't show up. It was this legacy of the old days of radio that allowed Long John to continue.

When he was too weak, he would sometimes go out in the middle of his own show and take a nap. His friends would keep up the banter until he woke up and came back on. Some days it seemed that he was practically living on the sofa in the lobby of WMCA.

On many mornings, when I got to work, I'd see Long John asleep on the sofa, where he had been dozing since his program went off the air. He was a tall, emaciated figure, with a pale gray pallor that let you know that "time's wingèd chariot" was drawing near. Some mornings he'd barely have the strength to pull his bone-thin, disheveled six-foot frame up from the sofa.

"Oh, it's *morning!*" he'd say in his weak, crackly voice.

Every now and then I'd beckon him to join me for the opening of my show. "Long John," I said, "I've got no one to start my show with. Come into the studio and sit with me."

I did it more out of kindness than anything else. I enjoyed carrying the opening of my show by myself with a half hour of talk before the guests came on. But I felt sorry for this old, wasted man. And so we'd play a little charade that both of us understood.

Long John would say, "Oh, I work so hard at night. Now you expect me to help you get your show going in the morning?"

And I'd respond, "But nobody does it better than you."

With that Long John would feel needed, and he would walk into my studio.

That's when the miracle took place. Every radio station has a red ON AIR sign that lights up when you're on the air. The minute that red light went on, there in front of me, as if by magic, appeared a strong, virile man whose voice had the resonance of a man in his thirties. His mind was razor-sharp, and he was strong and alive for whatever amount of time he stayed with me.

The minute he left the studio, though, his voice became thin and crackly, and he shriveled back up into a weak, wizened old man.

When he died, I went to his funeral. The thing that struck me was the devotion of his fans. There were dozens of little old ladies standing around his coffin, looking down at him with love in their eyes. That was the kind of hold that radio people have over their audiences.

Because of people like Long John, WMCA had a special aura. It was a place where you earned your stripes. But despite the talent the station attracted, WMCA was run like a mom-and-pop store. The owners, Ellen and Peter Straus, got personally involved in every decision, fiddling with this and that—a practice that some believe caused the station eventually to plummet from a rating of ninth in the city to near the bottom.

But during my years there WMCA was still an exciting place to be. Everybody in town knew where it was: "Number 57 on the dial," located at Fifty-seventh Street and Seventh Avenue. What most people didn't know, perhaps, was that the station derived its call letters—MCA—from the McAlpin Hotel, where the station had originally been located.

Talk radio has always been an important part of the rhythm of New York. New Yorkers love to hear the latest chat and gossip, just as they want to be seen and heard reading the right books and going to the right restaurants. So, if you're on the air talking about movies and shows and restaurants, you can make yourself a vital part of the city's life.

I found out just how important a show like mine could be during one of New York's blackouts. With all electrical power on the blink, the city was in complete chaos. Nothing was functioning. Yet publicists were fighting like crazy to get their clients on the air. It was a press agent's dream. Everyone in New York City was tuned in to the radio for information about the blackout, and any author or movie star who was on was sure to be listened to.

As a result, every guest booked for my talk show during the blackout managed to get to the studio *on time*, even though there were no elevators running and no electricity in the entire building. The generators on the roof enabled us to transmit the broadcasts, but there was no power for anything else. We did the shows by candlelight. It only proves to what length people will go to promote something.

There's a delicate symbiosis between press agents and talk show personalities that is hard to describe but very real. If press agents could be your best friends during a blackout, they were also quick to turn on you if you didn't play by their rules. That's what I discovered when I began to review plays as a second-night theater critic.

I managed to see everything that opened on Broadway

during the time I was reviewing plays at MCA, but it wasn't easy. It may look glamorous and fun, but it actually requires a lot of discipline. You have to go to obscure productions off-off-Broadway, as well as the glitzy hits that everyone's dying to see. To make matters worse you have to fight to get to the theater even in a blizzard or when you're not feeling good. The show must go on, and so must you. If you miss enough plays or don't do enough reviews, the theater publicists will simply stop sending you tickets. They'll send the tickets to someone who they know will show up and cover their shows.

As much as I loved reviewing plays, though, my stock-in-trade was interviews. While I was at WMCA, I managed to log fifty-two hundred hours of interviews with the famous and soon-to-be-famous. I can remember one unknown actress who was working in an off-Broadway play. Of all the actresses I'd interviewed, there was something magical about her that made her different from all the rest. Maybe it was because she was Meryl Streep!

But it wasn't the guests that I remember most fondly about WMCA. It was the paycheck. Whatever the drawbacks of the place, the station always paid my salary on time. That meant that every now and then Karl and I could indulge our passion for travel.

You have to understand right off the bat that Karl and I get along very, very well. That doesn't mean that we don't fight like cats and dogs and have big disagreements—because we do. Or that I'm not hard to live with—as I may be. Karl, on the other hand, is very easy to live with. He takes other people in stride so well that he could live with Attila the Hun and think he was a "nice guy."

This may sound wonderful, but a man who's *that* nice can sometimes drive you crazy. Especially when there's a crisis. That's when nice guys are at their worst. They may think there's nothing to worry about—even though you're almost having a heart attack!

What happened to us at Charles de Gaulle Airport in Paris, at the end of a wonderful vacation in France, illustrates my point. As I've mentioned, whenever we had a penny to spend, we'd spend it on travel. If we didn't have a penny, we'd put the plane tickets on our credit cards, look at each other with a shrug, and go anyway.

The trip to Paris was one of those trips—bought on faith and paid for on a wing and a prayer. We took the whole family along during the kids' summer vacation. J.J. was three or four at the time, Allison was studying to be a chef at the Culinary Institute of America, and Andrea was about to go off to Seattle to finish her last two years of high school and live with her father.

It was wonderful having the family all together, and we had a grand time seeing the sights and living on baguettes and Brie. Buoyed by so many satisfying, joyful experiences, we got to the airport with about an hour to spare before our charter flight home. We had timed the flight just right so that Andrea could get back to Seattle in time to start school and I could get back to my job at WMCA.

Karl dropped us off at the terminal and then handed me his passport and wallet so that I could check him through customs while he returned the rented car. Then he disappeared.

Everything went smoothly at the Air France check-in counter and customs. All we had to do was board the plane, and we'd be on our way home. Andrea could make her connection to Seattle, Allison could start school, and I could be back at work.

But where was Karl? It began to dawn on me that Karl was not going to make it. I knew we couldn't wait for him. We'd forfeit all our tickets if we missed the charter. Under the circumstances it was far better for one of us to miss the plane than for all of us to be stranded. But he had no passport and no money. How would he get along? What if something terrible had happened to him?

I tried not to panic. Maybe the Air France ticket agent

would hold his passport for him. In my best French I begged. I pleaded. I cajoled. But nothing moved him.

"We will not take anybody's passport," said the agent obstinately.

By now all the other passengers were on the plane, and I had no choice but to hustle the kids on board and try to console them.

"What's happened to Daddy?" wailed J.J. Even Allison and Andrea were getting distraught.

"I'm sure he'll be along any minute," I said.

Now I was no longer anxious. I was mad.

Meanwhile, Karl was back at Charles de Gaulle Airport going through his own crisis of sorts. He had been heading for the rent-a-car return when he ran out of gas on the *périphérique*—the beltway around the airport. He managed to back off a ramp going the wrong way and ended up parking the car in the middle of a street.

Luckily for Karl, a Frenchman with a cigarette stuck in his mouth came along on a little motorbike and gave him a ride to a gas station. Unluckily for Karl, it was closed. So was the next one, and the next, until finally he found one open and managed to buy a teacupful of petrol for 4.5 francs. That left him with about 10 francs. When he returned to the car, two gendarmes were standing there grimacing.

Karl has a surefire way of handling a crisis in a foreign country: Never, never speak the language. Play dumb, and you'll get away unscathed.

In English Karl said with a smile, "Fine, I'm glad you're here. I ran out of gas." Then he dumped the gas in the car, waved at them, and took off.

By the time he found the car return, he had twenty minutes left before flight time.

"This is really going to be tight," he said to himself. "Where's the bus?" he asked an attendant.

"On the corner," said the man.

The only problem was, Karl didn't have enough money

for the bus. He managed to explain his predicament to the bus driver, who gave him a ride anyway.

When he got to the terminal, he had just enough time to make a call to the gate, in the hope that they would hold the plane for him.

"What time does my plane leave?" he asked the agent.

"They're just ready to close the door," the man responded.

"My wife is on the plane," he yelled. "I have no passport, no wallet, nothing. Let me speak to my wife."

"But she's on the plane," the agent protested.

"Pull her off," Karl screamed.

Three minutes later the agent came back with me on the line. "Sally," said Karl, "the plane is leaving. Leave me money, leave me my passport, leave anything!"

"They won't let me," I said. "I can't talk now. My plane is leaving!" Then I hung up.

I was fuming. It was all clear to me now. This mess was all Karl's fault. "He's *always* late," I muttered to myself. "It's habitual. Why couldn't he just dump the car and run for it?"

With my rage increasing, I buckled the kids into their seats, dried their eyes, and got ready for a long flight to America.

The stewardess could see that we were upset, and she graciously tried to assuage us with a bottle of French wine. Unfortunately the plane jolted as she was pouring the wine and it spilled all over our clothes.

So there I was, stuck in a jammed airplane with three sticky, grumbling kids, and I still had to face the luggage rack at Kennedy Airport—alone!

Karl was all alone, too, but not for long. Once he discovered he was stuck in Paris, his creative mind started clicking. That's when he remembered Shirley.

Shirley was a luscious brunette who worked in public relations for Revlon. She had been introduced to us by a friend, and we had met her for lunch just a few days before. At lunch she had let it drop that she would be at the airport on the day we left, meeting her boss and the French ambassador, who were flying in on the Concorde.

Using that slim piece of information and the strength of our new friendship, Karl went looking for Shirley.

"Karl, what are you doing here?" she said with surprise.

"You're not going to believe this, Shirley," he said matter-of-factly. "Sally and the kids have left me."

"What do you mean?" she asked sympathetically.

"I missed the plane," he answered.

"Don't worry," she said. "Go down to Maxim's in the airport, eat some dinner, and after I welcome the ambassador, I'll meet you."

Karl didn't need any further invitation to make himself right at home. With his ten francs in his pocket, but with no tie and no credit cards, he waltzed into Maxim's and ordered the best meal on the menu. He ordered a twenty-five-dollar bottle of wine. He ordered dessert, and he actually sat there enjoying himself as he waited for Shirley.

In a predicament like this, a lot of people would be frustrated and panic-stricken. But not Karl. He reasons that if this is the situation God gives you, enjoy it! Have a great time!

His only really sticky moment came near closing time. It was eleven-thirty at night, and he was the last patron in the restaurant. The waiters kept buzzing around him, obviously trying to get him to leave. But he couldn't. He had to wait for Shirley in order to pay the bill. So he kept on drinking his wine until Shirley finally appeared at the door.

"Karl, I'm so sorry," she said breathlessly. "The ambassador wanted to have a meeting, and I couldn't get away."

After a few more pleasantries she paid the bill, and the two of them walked out into the cool Parisian night.

At the opposite side of the Atlantic, however, things looked even grimmer than I had expected. As our plane came in for a landing at Kennedy Airport, we were in the middle of a driving rainstorm. Somehow I had to collect the kids and the luggage and get Andrea to another terminal to catch her plane to Seattle.

Miraculously we made it, and I waved her good-bye and piled in a cab with J.J. and Allison and headed home.

I could have survived all that with just a little encouragement over the telephone. One eensy-weensy ring from Karl was all I needed. But I woke up the next morning, and still no phone call. I went to WMCA, and still no call.

The next day, and the next, there was *still* no phone call.

People were starting to get curious. "What happened to your husband?" they asked.

"I don't know," I answered. "I left him in Paris."

"Well, are you two getting a separation or what?"

Of course, I knew we weren't on the road to a breakup, but I said, "I have no idea. He's not around. And he hasn't called."

On the fourth day I was about to go on the air when the producer said, "You've got a long-distance call from Paris."

"I will *not* accept the call," I said firmly. In the back of my mind I figured if he could live three days without me, I could let him sweat now.

I repeated my order. "Do *not* accept the call."

The next day I was on the air when another producer put Karl's call through without telling me.

"Hi, honey," said Karl.

On the air, with all of New York listening, I answered, "Who is this?"

"It's Karl," he answered.

"Sorry, wrong number." And I hung up.

It's a good thing I did, too, because Karl was going to do something cute like give a weather report from Paris, which would have infuriated me even more.

On the sixth day I got another call—this time from someone at the American Embassy who claimed that my husband needed a passport. "Could you please wire the passport?" the man from the embassy asked.

"I'm sorry," I said. "I have no idea who you're talking about."

If you think that Karl was upset by all this, you're wrong. That's because he was living the high life in Shirley's apartment! It was in the classy Fourteenth Arrondissement, near the Champs-Élyseés. It turned out that Shirley had lent him a few hundred dollars to tide him over. Then she went away on a business trip, leaving Karl to explore Paris to his heart's content.

He had settled into being a "kept man," for heaven's sake, while I was busting my britches to earn a buck back home!

After a week of this nonsense, with the kids getting *seriously* concerned about Karl's absence, I finally decided I had had enough. The next call I accepted.

It was Karl. He was coming in on Icelandic Airlines and wanted me to wire him a ticket and passport and meet him at the airport.

I'd be waiting for him all right. My friend Harriet Norris drove me to the airport. I knew I could count on Harriet, because she's not only a good friend but also a savvy business executive who's skilled at negotiations. And boy, did I need a negotiator!

On the way to the airport I insisted she stop at a bakery.

"Why?" she asked incredulously.

"I want to buy a loaf of French bread."

Karl breezed through the gate and shouted gleefully, "There's my baby, waiting with Harriet!"

I walked up to him and whacked him over the head with the French bread. All the while I was shouting epithets in Spanish. The crumbs were flying all over the place, and a crowd started gathering around.

Karl just laughed.

To add insult to injury, he had a present for me: fur

mukluks that he bought in Iceland when the plane stopped over. The guy had spent a week in Paris, and instead of coming home with something classy, like expensive perfume, he had gotten me slippers!

Harriet, who was totally taken aback by the whole scene, had only one subdued comment: "I guess that's healthy for you to express your emotions."

It's a lucky thing that Karl and I know how to let off steam with each other because the pressures of our working lives create constant havoc.

Somehow our difficulties worsen whenever opportunity seems to knock. The bad news always seems to follow the good news.

CHAPTER EIGHT

Hitting Bottom

ALTHOUGH I WAS MAKING progress in radio, I had also always wanted to get back into television. Finally an opportunity came. Through a lucky series of circumstances I got my chance at WPIX, Channel 11, in 1976. Anchorwoman Pat Harper had left the station, and I was tapped for her 10:00 P.M. slot.

This was one of those rare instances when getting the job was easy. I had gotten a call one morning from Lester Lewis, an agent who handled everybody who was anybody in broadcasting.

"Sally, are you represented by anybody?" he asked.

"No," I answered.

"How about going down to Channel Eleven to do an audition?" he asked.

I didn't hesitate for a second. I immediately hopped a cab to Channel 11, read a little piece of news copy, and the next day the station called and said, "Okay, you're an anchorwoman."

That's all it took to catapult me to the ranks of the elite corps of New York TV anchors. At the time it struck me as more than a little ironic. From the time I had started in broadcasting I had gone through hundreds of interviews, dozens of auditions, and weeks of waiting to get little jobs that never went anywhere. Yet here it took no more than a half hour—twenty minutes for the cab ride and ten for the audition—to land a big job like anchorwoman in New York.

But that's how it is in broadcasting. As it turned out, it was the only time in my life that I got a job "overnight."

It was a thrilling prospect to be a TV anchorwoman in the country's number one market. I felt I was ready, and I looked forward to a great future on camera. But what I didn't know was that Pat Harper's departure was only temporary. With two years left in her contract, she had quit the station and moved to Spain with the promise that her job would be waiting for her when she returned.

The result was that as Pat Harper's "stand-in" at WPIX I spent the worst eight months of my broadcasting career. From the moment I stepped in the door, nothing I did was quite right. One day they changed my hairstyle. The next day it was the makeup or the clothes. They constantly replayed tapes of my anchoring sessions and then, like Monday morning quarterbacks, ripped them to shreds.

Day after day I was picked apart and beaten down without any clear direction or sense of support from the management. "Be stronger," I'd hear on Monday. "Be weaker," they'd say on Tuesday. "Be taller, be shorter, have fluffy hair, have straight hair." That was the way it went, for eight long months.

Now, in fairness to WPIX, I must say that television is a business of images. We all communicate certain things by the way we look and act. I know that, and I'm willing to adapt up to a point to whatever is commercially viable. But you shouldn't have to go along with the vicissitudes of someone else's whims.

Women in television have to put up with constant challenges to their images and their very egos. Christine Craft, the former television anchorwoman from Kansas City who took her station to court, made her name battling the bad guys in television who told her she was "too old, too unattractive and not deferential enough to men."

I faced the same kind of "image enhancing" at WPIX more than a decade ago, and it still rankles. What rankles even more is the way my job came to an end.

I happened to look up from my desk one day to see Pat Harper wandering around the studio. I figured she was back visiting her old friends and didn't give it another thought even after I saw her back again the next day. She continued this routine for a week or more, and then I began to notice that my colleagues were acting kind of furtive and funny. People seemed to be whispering among themselves and looking at me strangely.

Finally, after watching Pat move in and out of the station for two weeks, I asked the makeup man, "Why is she here?"

He wouldn't tell me. It wasn't long before the management called me in to give me the bad news: I was out and Pat was in. Just like that, I was back on the streets and out of a job. In sympathy, my co-host, Paul Blom, quit and went to San Diego.

My situation wasn't as desperate as it might have been, though. The smart move I had made was to keep my daytime job at WMCA during those months at WPIX. I may not have been too savvy about the fickleness of television, but I did know how to hedge my bets.

What I didn't bet on, though, was that there was more trouble ahead for us. This time it wasn't the job that threatened to defeat us. It was my mother's failing health.

The good news was that my various jobs provided us with a steady enough income that I could bring my mother up from Florida and we could be a family again.

The bad news was that she still needed to be in a nursing home. Dede had never recovered from the rape and her subsequent stroke. By the time we moved her to New York, she was confined to a wheelchair, unable to move her right hand or her right leg.

Her beautiful face was permanently frozen in a smiling expression. Oddly enough, she was able to laugh, but the only word that she could get out of her mouth was "Marvelous." As a result, we never could figure out how much she really understood. That was her tragedy of being locked in an immobile body.

An even greater problem was that the only caretaking facility that would take her on our limited budget was a city-run nursing home for the poor. We visited her all the time, but it was awful. Every time I visited, I had visions of Olivia de Havilland in the insane asylum in *The Snake Pit*. People were strapped to the walls; it was dirty all the time; the stench was overwhelming. It was really that bad.

But no matter how many tubes were in her, or how much pain she was in, or how much she disliked the place, Dede, with her limited capacity to express herself, never let on how she felt. It was just in her character. She was the kind of person who never showed unhappiness. Always positive and upbeat, she had the most wonderful, sweet nature in the world. In years past, if I had walked into her house at 2:00 A.M. and said, "Let's go on an adventure," she would have said, "Great, let's do it now!"

That's the way she was in the nursing home, too. I'd talk to her, and she'd respond by nodding her head and whispering, "Marvelous, marvelous."

But I knew it wasn't marvelous. Her eyes gave her away. She had the look of a frightened animal.

It was horrible to see her in that place and in such a helpless condition, and I was tormented by guilt. Month after month I tried to use every ounce of pull I had—which wasn't much—to have her shifted someplace else. Nothing seemed to work.

It didn't help that I knew Dede forgave me. She would have forgiven me if I had killed her. She loved me so much that no matter what I did, she would have said, "Sally has a reason."

That's why it was so difficult to tolerate what she was

going through. This dear, sweet woman, who had given so much to me, was suffering, and I could do nothing to help.

It was bad enough that she was living in a virtual "snake pit." But then she was diagnosed as having ovarian cancer, and an operation seemed to be the only remedy.

Right then and there I should have screamed, "No, you can't do that to my mother!" I should have remembered what had happened so many years before, when my father had languished after useless operations. But I didn't. Instead, I listened to the doctors and allowed them to operate.

The operation was more than Dede's body could bear. Although she survived, her health deteriorated much more rapidly after the surgery.

The only silver lining is that Dede spent the last year of her life in a wonderful Catholic nursing home, Mary Manning Walsh, just a few blocks from our apartment. It was a loving, beautiful environment, filled with caring people and fresh, clean smells. For that I will always be grateful.

But the truth was, her operation, too, was useless and she was dying.

Every day I expected the dreaded phone call to come with the news that she had died, but week after week she clung to life. As the weeks went on, it grew harder and harder to visit. My job and the kids demanded a lot of me, and quite honestly, there's a point, as you're waiting for someone to die, when you become lax about going to visit —especially if the sick person can't communicate. I know this may sound hard and heartless, but I'm just telling it like it was for me.

Even as I write this, I am riddled by guilt because of the devotion Dede had given me as a child. I know it was not my finest hour. Although I can give excuses, I can't erase from my mind the memory of Dede alone and dying in the nursing home while I gave priority to the pressures of my job and children. Despite all the advice I give on the air, I still am at a loss for answers about this sort of family problem.

In the end the best I could do for Dede was give her a sendoff she would have rejoiced over. When she died in the summer of 1978, instead of giving her a funeral I invited our closest friends to the apartment for a bon voyage party. In the center of the table I put a gigantic bowl filled with cherries. It was a symbol of the way Dede saw life—sweet, rosy, and ripe for adventure—and the way she would have wanted us to think of her always. All evening long we told marvelous Dede stories, and when the guests finally left, I closed the door and tried to cry.

A part of me has been trying to cry ever since.

From that point on our lives began to crumble. Not long after Dede died, Karl opened a restaurant called the Wine Press, which gradually began to drain us of all our energy *and* my broadcasting money.

To make matters worse, in 1981 I was hit with another terrible blow. My job at WMCA—the financial lifeline that had sustained us for five years in New York City—was abruptly canceled.

I got the news in one of the newspapers.

"Sally has not kept up with the times," said a comment in the media section.

After all those years it wasn't the most gracious way to bid someone adieu. But by now you get the drift about the way things work in broadcasting. What's here today is usually gone tomorrow. How any of us has the fortitude to stick with it is as much a mystery to me as it is to you. All I can say is that you have to want it so badly you're willing to be fired for it—over and over again.

But it doesn't make it any easier to accept. I still had to cope with the rejection and the stinging personal indictment in the press. There's no way you can completely gird yourself for derogatory reports in the newspapers. Some celebrities solve the problem by not reading the things that are written about them. Others try, as I do, to be realistic and understand that everyone in the public eye is subject to negative reviews at one time or another. It's simply a fact of celebrity life.

Even with such rational thinking, though, it's not easy to shrug it off. In your head you may know it's pointless to let criticism get you down. But in your heart you feel it.

My reaction was to do what I always do when I've been fired: I had a "pity party." I lay down on the yellow divan in my living room, put a stack of old Judy Garland records on the stereo, and spaced out for three days straight. The family knew better than to try to talk me out of my misery. They just let me wallow in depression, until I got sick of being sorry for myself.

On the third day I wasn't getting any better, so I climbed off the divan and announced, "Okay, let's go out and start to find a job!"

At five years old, with mother and brother, Steven, I was expecting a life of class and comfort.

Below, all the world was my stage as a teenager (right) opposite Geraldine Page in *The Empress.* I dyed my hair black for the role at the Westport Playhouse in Connecticut.

Above left, twenty years old in my Lana Turner pose. Unlike Lana, I was *not* discovered overnight. It took more than thirty years for me to make it. *Right,* Karl Soderlund, the man who has always believed in me and dreamed my dreams, at the mike in his Air Force radio days.

Below, I thought I was a hot ticket in Puerto Rico in the late sixties, when I hosted an English-language radio show. These days, the hair is still blond, but my false eyelashes are a thing of the past.

Above, on *A.M. Miami* I got the chance to meet my hero, Jean Shepherd, face-to-face. As a young girl, night after night I listened to Shepherd weave his magical spells on radio, and before long the broadcast "monkey" had climbed on my back.

Poet Rod McKuen is what a star ought to be. He once flew to Miami from the Coast at his own expense to help me make a pilot for a new talk show. The show never got off the ground—but McKuen's gallant gesture has left me in his debt.

Above, Maurice Tunick (right), the creator of NBC's Talknet, a new radio talk network, gave me the big break I needed to be on a track for radio success. As the "Dear Abby" of the airwaves, I started giving advice to callers across the country in 1982. Karl, our son, J.J., and I pose with Maurice, who is now a top radio executive with ABC.

Today the ABC Radio Networks carries my radio show, *Sally Jessy Raphaël,* from coast to coast. For the cost of a phone call, anyone from a teen to a grandparent can call me to share his or her deepest secrets, longings, and fears. Every night of the week I'm ready to listen.

Top, here I am in St. Louis on the set of *In Touch With Sally Jessy Raphaël,* before we changed the show's name and went national. The pantsuits and shoot-from-the-hip aggressiveness went out the door along with the name change. *Center,* a more ladylike Sally—outfitted in dresses and quietly sympathetic to her guests—talks with a member of the studio audience. *Bottom,* with Phil Donahue in St. Louis. Phil heard one of my radio broadcasts and touted me to Multimedia, which also produces his show. Over the years, he has continued to support me behind the scenes. When I got my Emmy award in 1989 and stood shaking onstage, through the fog of the spotlights I was comforted to see the beaming faces of Phil and his wife, Marlo Thomas, smiling encouragement.

Talking about life and love with heartthrob Julio Iglesias.... I didn't even spill the wine!

Right, my days may be filled with TV tapings, but my nights are consumed by radio. One of my luxuries was doing the radio show in my pajamas on remote two days a week from the hotel in St. Louis.

Below, in a rare subdued moment with the studio audience in New Haven, after the production of *Sally Jessy Raphaël* moved from St. Louis in 1987.

Just so we won't get bored, we bought ourselves a bed and breakfast inn in Bucks County, Pennsylvania. It's called the Isaac Stover House, in the town of Erwinna. Our very first guests were a sweet elderly couple in their seventies who turned out to be "shacking up!"

Karl and I know that the real secret to our success is our togetherness. He's my chief cheerleader, promoter, and best friend.

Emmy and me. Fairy tales *can* come true, and it happened to me in 1989 when I won TV's top prize for best talk-show host. That was also the year my show took a great leap forward and moved production to New York. I guess you could say I've finally arrived!

CHAPTER NINE

On the Verge

FOR YEARS I had the sense I was just on the verge of "making it" in broadcasting.

Nothing sums up my expectations better than my experience applying for jobs at WOR radio in New York. For as long as I can remember, WOR has been the number one talk radio station in the country. So, naturally, whenever I was out of a job, it was the first place I hit.

In fact, I had my sights set on WOR back in the early sixties, when I first met Karl in Puerto Rico.

"What's the top for you?" Karl had asked. "What's the Olympics of broadcasting for your kind of style?"

"WOR," I said without hesitation.

"Okay," he said. "I'll get you a job at WOR."

I just laughed, but that only spurred Karl on. Year after year we sent samples of my broadcasts to the station, and year after year we heard nothing.

Even that didn't stop us from trying. On one trip north from Puerto Rico, we had dropped in at WOR to try to sell ourselves. We explained to the program director that our specialty was talk radio and that Karl and I were on radio in San Juan.

"We're just what WOR needs," we said. "A nice young couple who can play off one another."

"Sorry," he said. "We don't change our programming

119

very much, and we don't have anything open. But if ever anything opens, we'll be glad to give you a call."

We took that to mean he'd call us the next day. Then he added, "By the way, would you like to see the Fitzgeralds do their show?"

With eager anticipation—expecting that such a gesture meant we were practically in—we went into the studio. There were Ed and Pegeen Fitzgerald, the comfortable twosome who made chatting over morning coffee a radio institution. In 1937 they had begun broadcasting their banter over breakfast on WOR, and they had been on the air ever since.

As we walked out of the studio, I said with excitement, "Karl, the guy likes us. We're in. Did you notice how old that couple was? That must mean that we'll take their place. I just *know* it."

We waltzed out of WOR certain that we were on the verge of taking over the Fitzgeralds' slot. In fact, we weren't.

Five years later, in 1969, we knocked on WOR's door again and got the same kind of welcome. That was the time we ended up at the station with the bullet holes in Hartford.

Five years after that, I had been fired from *A.M. Miami*, and once again we went job hunting in New York. As usual we hit WOR, which by now had a new program director.

"We've talked to your predecessor," we said confidently. "Here's a tape of some of our shows. We can do singles; we can do it as a couple; we're ready to go. We're just what WOR needs: young talk!"

"Have you seen the Fitzgeralds?" asked the program director.

"Yes," I said enthusiastically.

"Well, come and watch them again," he beckoned. "They're on the air right now."

By now Ed Fitzgerald was sitting in a wheelchair.

"They're wheeling him in!" I whispered to Karl. "The Fitzgeralds are on their last legs. We're going to be here in a month."

Almost in unison we started whistling "Happy Days Are Here Again." We whistled that for several more years before we had the nerve to try again.

This time it was 1981, and I had just been fired by WMCA. Despite the firing, though, we were sure that *now* we would be shoo-ins at WOR. After all, my name was known in New York, and I had more than twenty years of broadcasting under my belt.

Karl and I showed the program director our book and then asked casually, "By the way, how are the Fitzgeralds?"

We peered through the studio glass, and there was Ed Fitzgerald *asleep* in front of the microphone. He had dozed off on the air while reading *Variety*, the show business newspaper!

When we first saw them, they had been in their fifties. Now they were in their seventies, and *we* were even seeming a little "mature"!

Ed died in 1982, but Pegeen stayed on the air on another station until her death in 1989! WOR had let her go in 1983 because, as she said, "the station told me I had lived too long." Ironically, she may have outlived her usefulness to radio, but not to her fans. One elderly widow left Pegeen $2.2 million in her will because of their mutual love of animals!

As for me, I may have thought I was on the verge of making it at WOR, but again, I came away empty-handed. What's more, for the next year and a half, beginning in 1981 when I was fired from WMCA, I went into the biggest slump of my career. I approached station after station with my star-studded résumé, and station after station turned thumbs down. For eighteen long months I batted zero.

At first I forged ahead, believing that since I had

worked for a top ten station in the country's number one broadcasting market, my ability to land a job was certain. I knew that basically broadcasting is a numbers game. Somewhere, in the big Personnel Office in the sky, every broadcaster is assigned an unwritten number, based on the selling power of the city his station is in. The bigger the market, the better your chances of getting another job —supposedly.

Whenever I'd go to a convention and meet another broadcaster, we'd automatically size each other up in terms of the market we were in. If someone said, "I'm in Pittsburgh," I knew immediately that he was in market nine. I had moved from market number fifteen in Miami to number one in New York, and I thought I was pretty hot stuff.

But month after month, as I went without work, my self-esteem began to plummet. We put ads in the trade press, expecting to hear from some station in one of the top ten markets. When station owners didn't call us, we called them. But no one wanted me. After the third month we sent out feelers to radio stations in the top twenty markets. Still no answer. After six months we hit the top fifty markets.

By the time nine months passed, I knew I was in trouble. I began to think I would never find work again. I even started believing all the negative things that had been said about me over the years. Maybe the newspapers had been right. Maybe I couldn't keep up with the current radio trends, here or anywhere else.

What hurt even more was the immediate rejection by the press agents whose clients I had once interviewed and promoted. The minute I was fired by WMCA, the theater tickets stopped coming and the invitations to various screenings and parties dried up. It wasn't that I loved the night life and the frenetic activity of New York's social scene. Truthfully I never had much stomach for it. Other than going to the theater, I had always opted to stay home with my family.

But emotionally it was hard to take the fact that overnight I had become "nobody." Like the "playboy of the Western world," I had once been a hero, and now the crowd had turned on me and I was a pariah.

The only thing that kept me sane during this period was the rhythm and special madness of our family life on Seventy-second Street. With an endless assortment of children and animals living under our roof, there was always some absurd crisis that gave comic relief to my problems.

None was more absurd than the day our jet black jumbo poodle, named Fame, walked out the apartment door and disappeared for an entire morning. To me, the incident has become a parable of my life in broadcasting. Maybe it's because I've always had a special attachment to fame, in all its forms!

We had gotten the dog in Puerto Rico, and for a while we had two dogs: Fame and a dachshund named Fortune. We gave Fortune away and were left with Fame; that tells you something about our sense of priorities.

Fame was a rare creature, a huge Argentine breed that was the size of a St. Bernard. We loved him dearly, but he was too big to take with us on various family outings. That's how it happened that we left Fame behind one weekend when we went off on a trip. With him in the apartment was fifteen-year-old Alexandra, the daughter of a good friend of mine from Puerto Rico. Alexandra was one of those kids who happened to drop into our lives for a year or two and become part of the family.

Since I didn't want to leave Alexandra and Fame unattended, I had asked my friend Sandy Keay, who lived in New Jersey, to come stay and look after them. Actually it wasn't Alexandra I was worried about. It was Fame.

Early Saturday morning Sandy was awakened by a loud buzz over the intercom.

"Your dog has just run out the door!" said the door-man.

As it turned out, Alexandra had gone to the laundry room, leaving the door ajar. Fame, seeing his opening, walked down the hall, threw himself against the door to the stairwell, climbed down the stairs, and ran through the lobby before anyone could do anything about it. The front doors to the building open automatically, so Fame just kept going.

The last the doorman saw him, he was trotting down Seventy-second Street, probably singing to himself, "Free again, I'm free again."

When Sandy heard from the doorman that the dog had disappeared, she threw a coat over her pajamas and raced out the door to look for him. Like a maniac, she ran up and down the streets of the Upper East Side, asking every-one she saw, "Have you seen a dog?"

Finally, in desperation, she spotted a police box and called for help. But when the cops pulled up in the squad car, they were less than thrilled.

"Lady, in New York City you don't ring the police if your dog is gone."

"Please," she begged. "I'm watching this dog for some-one. You've *got* to help me."

It must have been a slow day at the precinct because the cops put her in the squad car and then drove up and down the streets, canvasing the neighborhood.

At every block Sandy stuck her head out the squad car and yelled, "Fame! Fame!"

After a fruitless search the cops dropped her off on the street and left her to her wanderings. Four hours later, demoralized, she returned to the house. But when she opened the door to the apartment, there, to her astonish-ment, was Fame. He jumped on her with delight and started barking with joy.

Sandy, of course, was more confused than ever. Was it all a dream? Was she going nuts? Had the dog been in the apartment all the time, while she had searched the streets for hours in her pajamas?

Later the police filled her in. Soon after they had left Sandy on the street, Fame had trotted by. They brought him home in the squad car, and the doorman had let him into the apartment.

Sandy was so overwhelmed by the whole experience that the minute she saw Fame, she just sat down and sobbed.

When we returned from our weekend trip and heard about Sandy's ordeal, I started laughing and crying at the same time. Her search for Fame was the story of my life! *I* might as well have been in the squad car, yelling out, "Fame! Fame!"

But unfortunately the other fame was never going to be delivered to my door the way the dog had been. Instead, I seemed doomed to a life of anonymity, in the midst of New York's broadcasting riches. With no job to sustain me, fame seemed even more elusive than ever.

Karl, of course, did his best to try to keep my spirits up. But the truth was, he had his mind on other kinds of spirits.

While I was still employed at WMCA, Karl got it into his head to open a wine bar on the Upper East Side. The idea sounded terrific. We'd have a nice little restaurant where people could drop in after work and have a relaxing glass of wine and a bite of cheese. It would be a romantic rendezvous, a comfortable gathering place, which would be a haven from the hustle and bustle of the city. We had seen such places in Europe, and Karl was sure the idea would take off in New York.

What's more, if it worked, we would have ultimate security from the broadcasting business, a solid income to fall back on if the rug was pulled out from under us. To finance the undertaking, we got together a bunch of friends and acquaintances who put up a few thousand dollars each. To decorate the place, we staged a modern-day barn raising, inviting our friends to help paint, sew linen napkins and tablecloths, and hang paintings of the bucolic French countryside.

With that tenuous beginning, and with very little knowledge of what we were getting into, we opened up the Wine Press, a stucco-front bistro with Gothic windows on First Avenue.

To help set up the wine list, we called in as a consultant our friend Ron Kapon, who is a noted authority on the subject. I had first met Ron, who prides himself on being America's worst-dressed man, on a bus in the south of Spain. The bus stopped for a moment, and there appeared a man wearing Bermuda shorts, terrible shoes, terrible socks, and a terrible shirt.

I whispered to my traveling companion, "Number one, he's American. Number two, he will head straight for me."

I was right. He immediately sat himself down behind me and started up an animated conversation.

From that moment on, we became fast friends. We're so close, in fact, that every year for the past ten years, Ron has proposed marriage to me at least four times a year—even though he knows Karl and I are inseparable. Some guys just don't take no for an answer.

But that's the way Ron is. He's my number-one fan, and he'll drop anything to help me and Karl out in a pinch. Unfortunately, even his superb wine list couldn't save the Wine Press.

From the moment we opened the door in 1979 it was a disaster. For starters, we discovered that our concept was off base. A wine bar wouldn't make it because America does not have a pub mentality. American people go home from work. Then they get dressed and go out to dinner. They do not stop by their clubs to chat and gossip with their friends.

We opened with 150 kinds of wine, sold by the glass,

and 30 kinds of cheeses. But within the first week or two the wine was spoiling and the cheese was rotting. These days wine bars rely on a gadget known as the Cruvinet, a wine dispenser that prevents spoilage. But few people in this country knew about the Cruvinet at the time—and certainly not us.

Karl was at his wit's end trying to generate business. Up to now his only restaurant experience had been as a waiter in that Italian restaurant in Connecticut, and you remember how that turned out!

He quickly hired a chef and started to serve dinner, and the restaurant limped along. Meanwhile, Karl was putting in fourteen to fifteen hours a day to keep the business going. Every day, instead of a triumph, there was some new tragedy. On Christmas Eve, for example, when other people were home with their families, we had to stay open to serve the three people who wandered in for dinner. On top of that we had to coddle the disgruntled employees, who didn't want to be there on a holiday either.

Karl tried everything to make it work. He first served lunch; then he canceled lunch. He tried Sunday brunch but got the price down so low that we were selling the brunch lower than the cost of the food.

Money was leaving the place faster than you could say "greenbacks." For one thing, the waiters were eating the profits.

Consider the creamy chocolate "ganache" cake that Karl served for dessert. The cakes cost Karl ten dollars each, and he'd cut them into eight slices. To break even, he had to sell at least five slices at two dollars each. That way he'd be left with no more than three pieces for a minimum profit of six dollars. But one minute he'd go into the kitchen and see his full profit sitting on a plate, and then the next minute he'd turn around and there would be only *two* pieces sitting there! A waiter had eaten a piece!

But the waiters were the least of our problems. There

were endless demands for money, from unimaginable sources. First the garbageman raised his rates because our garbage went from four bags to five.

"That'll be fifty dollars more a week," said the garbageman. "Cash."

"I'll just use another garbageman," said Karl.

But there was no other garbageman, and Karl had to ante up the increase. What Karl didn't know was that there was one garbageman for First Avenue, another for Second, and so on. Not only the garbageman but the linen man and the cigarette man each had corners on the market. To make matters worse, there was a purveyor for things you didn't even need.

One day I was in the restaurant lending a hand when a portly man came in and announced, "I'm the parsley man."

"But we're trying to serve some French country food here, and we don't need parsley," I protested.

"Oh, yes, you do," said the man. "*Everybody* needs parsley."

All of a sudden it dawned on me why all across America you see little sprigs of parsley scattered across people's plates. Is it because Americans hunger for parsley? Or is it because there are people who control the parsley market and have a way of pressuring the restaurateurs?

We were naïve, to put it mildly.

Month after month Karl managed to keep the place going, always hoping it would take off. But the Wine Press was pressing *us* to the limit. Karl was getting three and four hours of sleep every night, and the only way we could spend time with him was to help out at the restaurant. To keep the family together, we held all sorts of celebrations at the place, such as J.J.'s birthday parties and my brother's wedding. You name it, we celebrated it—just to be together.

Financially the place was drawing us deeper and deeper into debt. I started pouring my broadcasting money into the venture, and before long we were back living on credit cards again. What hurt even more than the drain on our resources was the gossip. A few of our friends and investors, who knew it was a cash business, had hinted that we must be taking money out of the till and living off it. "There's plenty of cash around," people whispered. "I'll bet they're siphoning it off."

Yet here I was, taking my hard-earned broadcasting money and putting it *in* the till. It cut me to the quick to think that people believed I was making a profit when I lost infinitely more than they did.

The restaurant may have drained us of cash, but it did provide us with an endless store of daily dramas. I can't share most of them with you because I believe in the unwritten law that says that bartenders, manicurists, and cabdrivers "don't talk." Many secrets were learned over a wine bar at three in the morning, and every secret is completely safe with me—except one.

Karl was sitting in the restaurant with the chef one morning, waiting for a delivery. The door was open, and in walked a nicely dressed middle-aged woman who asked politely, "Can I use the rest room?"

"Sure, it's downstairs," he said.

Karl went back to his conversation with the chef when he heard the woman say aloud, "I don't think I'll go down to the rest room. I think I'll go right here."

With that, she began to urinate—right on the floor in front of him.

"Don't do that! Don't do that here!" yelled Karl.

She didn't stop until a large puddle had formed at her feet.

"There are a hundred restaurants in this neighborhood. Why did you have to go here? *Please*, lady!" screamed Karl.

"I feel better now," she said. And she turned and walked out the door.

The Wine Press may have been an albatross, but inadvertently it also became my salvation. As my months of joblessness rounded into a new year, the only way I could keep my mind off my predicament was to help Karl around the restaurant. Often the "help" I provided was to chat with the patrons and keep the atmosphere light and friendly.

Soon I noticed a very attractive bachelor who came into the restaurant on a regular basis. More often than not, every time he came in he and I bantered back and forth. And the more we talked, the more we seemed to have in common. He knew lots of celebrities, many of whom I had interviewed. But I never said anything about my background or how depressed I was at being out of a job. Instead, I'd engage him in a personal game of broadcasting trivia to while away the time.

"You're so good at this!" I exclaimed one day. "Tell me, what do you do for a living?"

"I'm with NBC radio," he said casually.

My heart leaped into my throat. I had been hustling from station to station, trying to make contacts, while this man had been right under my nose for months!

"There's my pigeon," I said to myself. "There's my target. He's the guy who's going to get me out of this place!"

I ran straight into the kitchen to tell Karl. "Karl, the pigeon is outside!"

"What pigeon?" said Karl. He was so busy working on a soufflé that he couldn't be bothered listening to me.

I ran back to the man's table, sat down, and introduced myself. "Listen, I know this is a terrible thing to ask, but I'm a broadcaster, and I wonder if I could come see you and give a proposal for a new show?"

"Of course," he said. "Here's my card."

From the dark depths of my soul the sun suddenly came up, the bells began to chime, and fireworks started to go off.

Just around the corner, it seemed, was a very big deal.

My new friend's name was Walter Sabo, and he was

indeed with NBC. Karl and I went in to see him, and his office was everything I thought it would be. Walter's shelves were littered with toys. In fact, there was a ceramic frog in the bottom of the mug he gave me for coffee. How could a man like that *not* be on my side?

He listened intently to the presentation Karl and I made for a new program, and I got wonderful vibrations from him. Again the excitement started welling inside me. I could tell we were on the way. Selling NBC on an idea wasn't going to be easy, but this looked like a green light to me. Walter was extremely encouraging and told me to call back in two weeks.

Those were the nail-bitingest two weeks of my life. At this point, I was so eager for work that I was ready to take *anything*, even a radio job in market 199. I would have packed up the kids or even gone alone if I had to, though that would have been awful for me at that stage of my life.

But now, suddenly, there was hope for something really big. Here, maybe, I could have a shot at NBC. It seemed too good to be true.

In fact, it *was* too good to be true. Two weeks later I called back to find out that Walter Sabo had left NBC. I hurriedly did some detective work and tracked him down. When I found him, he was reassuring.

"Don't worry," he said. "I passed your idea along. Go and make the same presentation to Chuck Renwick at NBC."

A month later Karl and I made the same presentation to Chuck Renwick, and he, too, was very hospitable and encouraging.

"Call me in two weeks," he said with a smile.

Two weeks later Chuck was no longer at NBC.

Now it's true that work in TV is rather unstable. But the chances of such a rapid turnover in *any* executive position is pretty slim. Still, those were the kinds of cards I'd been dealt all my life.

Luckily, Chuck, too, had passed along my idea for a

show to an NBC executive. So, once again, Karl and I went in to make yet another pitch. At this point, though, the prospect of a job with NBC was beginning to look hopeless. No matter how receptive the executives seemed, we couldn't be sure they would be there the next week. Karl and I went home wondering what our next step would be.

That's when we got the call. Maurice Tunick, a top executive at NBC, wanted to meet us for lunch at Charley O's, a popular watering hole near the NBC studios. His boss, Morrie Trumble, would be there, too.

"Nobody calls you to have lunch if they don't like your idea," I said to Karl, trying to buoy myself up.

But as I walked into Charley O's, I was singing a different tune. It was from *A Chorus Line*: "I really need this job. Please God, I need this job. I've got to get this job."

The atmosphere at Charley O's didn't help my mood. The restaurant was a real broadcast hangout, and Maurice Tunick's table might as well have been right in the middle of Grand Central Station. People kept coming up to him and shaking hands and patting him on the back.

In between the comings and goings, Maurice made it very clear right from the start that NBC had decided *not* to do the show Karl and I had suggested to him. Once I realized the show was nixed, my mind went out of focus. Instead, I concentrated on the menu. I hadn't had a good restaurant lunch in a long time, so I decided that if someone was stupid enough to take me to lunch to tell me he wasn't going to do the show, I might as well eat sirloin instead of hamburger.

I ordered a double martini and a very expensive lunch and promptly forgot most of the rest of the conversation.

On the way out the door Maurice gave me a big hug and said, "Then we'll see you in Washington?"

"What do you mean, you'll see me in Washington?" I said.

"Sally, all through lunch we've been discussing the fact

that you're going to do a test for a new network talk show that we want you to do. You're doing the test on the Fourth of July in Washington."

So, on July 4, 1982, Karl and I flew down to Washington with Maurice Tunick for my "test."

If nothing else, the experience was a test of my ingenuity. The NBC-owned station in Washington, WRC, was known for political talk. That was about as far removed from my world as the Ayatollah. I hadn't done news since WINS, and I couldn't even tell you who was secretary of the treasury. Yet here I was, about to go on the air in Washington, D.C., the political talk capital of the world!

"They're gonna stone me out of the place," I said to Karl.

Then I went to work. Instead of talking about politics and politicians, I did what I do best. I zeroed in on people's lives and what the Fourth of July meant to them personally.

"It's the Fourth of July, a time for family gatherings," I said. Then I opened the phone lines and got people to stop thinking about politics and start thinking about themselves and their families.

The test worked. People started phoning in like crazy and pouring out their hearts and souls. The next thing I knew, I was hired!

Not only was I hired, but I was hired for New York—for the NBC radio network! I would be starting a show on a brand-new syndicated talk network that came to be known as Talknet.

Talknet was to have an advice format. People would call in, and I'd be the "Dear Abby" of the airwaves. Along with me, Maurice wanted someone who could give financial advice. I put him on to Bruce Williams, whom I had worked with at WMCA. Together we gave advice on the two things Freud said people are most interested in: money and love.

Talknet went on the air in the fall of 1982 with twenty

stations. Bruce was on live from eight to eleven at night, and I followed him from eleven to two. Then the network "flipped" our shows and rebroadcast them into the wee hours of the morning. So every night people could listen to me and Bruce for six hours each if they wanted to stay up that late.

Some people obviously did. From the moment it went on the air, Talknet was golden, and it continued to be golden for the five years I did my show for NBC. By 1987 more than three hundred stations were on the network carrying my program.

What's more, Talknet established me as a top female radio broadcaster and gave me a radio name nationally. My salary doubled, tripled, and quadrupled, and as the money and accolades rolled in, I began to feel good about myself as a broadcaster.

Not only that, but night after night at the NBC studios, I found myself in the thick of show business monkey business. My show originated from the eighth floor of 30 Rockefeller Plaza, and from the very first day I went in to check out the studio, I knew I was in for a rollicking good time.

I was still a little nervous about this new job with NBC, so before I took my first look at my studio, I stepped into the eighth-floor ladies' room to give myself the once-over.

As I stood in front of the mirror to comb my hair, I looked in the mirror and realized that I was standing next to a gorilla.

"Just play it straight," I said to myself, "This is show business, and this is serious. Don't make a joke. Don't do anything. Just stand there combing your hair."

Every crazy thing you ever read or heard about show business came to me in that one moment standing in front of the ladies' room mirror next to a gorilla.

The gorilla didn't say a word to me. She was busy adjusting her gorilla head and combing her matted hair with a pick. A few minutes later the gorilla left and went down the hall to rehearse for *Saturday Night Live*.

In the ensuing years, every time there was a break in my show, I'd go out in the hall to stretch my legs and find myself in the company of assorted coneheads, gorillas, and gladiators who had poured out of the studio where *Saturday Night Live* rehearsed on Friday nights.

To make matters worse, I could see them through the glass door of my studio even when I was on the air. Some distraught caller would be telling me on the air, "Sally, my life is over, please help me," and out of the corner of my eye I could see a hilarious parade of weirdos go waltzing by.

Alas, all good things must come to an end. I was in the midst of contract negotiations with NBC in 1987, and was just about to sign up for another few years, when I was told that NBC had decided to pull out of the radio network business. It had nothing to do with me or the show and everything to do with the temper of the times. The big broadcasting giants like NBC were crumbling, and crumbling fast. Apparently, it was no longer financially feasible for NBC to operate a far-flung radio network.

So the NBC radio network was up for sale. It was a black day for radio.

Deals were being struck right and left, but all of them seemed to leave me out in the cold. The new owners of the network offered me a deal that was easy to refuse: a cut in salary in exchange for some stock options.

"If the broad doesn't like it, then we'll get another broad," my agent was told.

The "broad" didn't like it. Eventually I happily signed on with the ABC radio network, where Maurice Tunick, the creator of Talknet, had moved. It's also a good thing I didn't take the stock options, because a few months later, the market fell apart.

But in an even stranger twist of fate the manager of my

show came to me and said, "By the way, the ABC network sold your show for syndication in New York."

"Who bought it?" I asked.

"WOR," he answered. "Bob Bruno, the station's general manager, sealed the deal."

As it happened, this switch occurred not long after Pegeen Fitzgerald died. I looked at Karl, and he looked at me, and we burst out laughing.

"We *finally* made it to WOR!" I said.

CHAPTER TEN

Talking My Way to the Top

RADIO MAKES ME FEEL wanted and needed.

When I'm on the air giving advice, I have a gut identification with my audience, and they with me. Marshall McLuhan was right when he called radio a "hot" medium. It's visceral. It satisfies the senses. As you hear radio, you see the pictures with your mind. In a way, you smell it; you can *feel* it deep inside.

Television has to filter through your eyes. It's cold and analytical. As a result, you may admire Jane Pauley, you may like to laugh at Johnny Carson, but you don't *need* them. The great radio people have been needed. A listener's day wasn't complete if he didn't hear Godfrey or Long John or Barry Gray.

I know that there are certain people—and I hope their number is legion—who need me on radio. There are people in hospitals, people who can't sleep, people who are dying for lack of love, and teenagers with uncompleted homework who probably shouldn't be listening at all who tune in to my show for solace.

Not long ago a lady who was dying of cancer called me on the air from her hospital bed. After that I called her back night after night just to chat with her. I really had nothing much to say, but I wanted to keep her spirits up.

Then one day her friend called to tell me the woman

had passed on. But before she died, she told her friend, "For goodness' sake, call Sally and tell her she made my final days!"

It's people like that who keep me going.

A friend from vaudeville once told me, "Never give up your night job." He said it as a caveat to keep me from falling on my face financially.

That doesn't mean that there aren't days I'd like to chuck it. There isn't a night that goes by that, like every writer who goes to a typewriter, like every dancer who prepares for a performance at the ballet, I don't take a deep breath and say, "Oh, my, would I *love* to go to bed, would I love to have a glass of wine, would I love to eat dinner, would I love to see a Broadway show."

All this is out for me. That's because five nights a week from seven to ten I have to be at the radio studio or at home with a set of earphones on my head to take calls from listeners all over the country. That's what I've done for nearly a decade, first with Talknet and now with the ABC radio network.

Just imagine what that's like. You can't go to a movie, or have friends over for dinner, or even read a book. When you finish a day of taping for television, you're dog tired, and you still can't relax. You have to be "on" for three more hours. That's the way it's been every single solitary weekday for almost ten years.

But then I put on those earphones, the red light goes on, I'm on the air, and somebody who needs me calls. When that happens, suddenly the fatigue of the day drains away, and it's all worthwhile.

As a call comes in, my mind becomes focused, and I go into an almost hypnotic trance, concentrating on the problem at hand and how I can help the caller solve it. It's as though there are just two of us—two good friends—in the room and we're sharing our deepest problems. The fact that millions of people across the country are eavesdropping on this conversation is irrelevant. All that's important to me is what's going on at the moment.

Romance still heads the list of questions on people's minds, and when it comes to love, I'm a hardheaded realist. I try to help people deal with the practical aspects of their romantic problems and leave fantasy to the fairy tales.

That's how I helped a Wisconsin dairy farmer snare a bride. I got a call one night from a man in Wisconsin who said he owned thirty head of cattle. I let him talk about himself for a few minutes and then asked, "What's your problem?"

He was forty-one years old, he said, and he had never had a date. A friend in town was going to fix him up with a girl, but since it was his first date, he really needed to know what to do to make a good impression.

There was something about the sound of his slow, steady voice that was endearing. I loved him—instantly. The mother in me wanted to be absolutely sure this sweet, determined man had a wonderful time on his first date.

So I said, "It's important to look neat. Be sure you wear a clean pair of jeans. If you've only got dirty ones, wash them!"

Now, as I told him this, I could picture people all across America thinking, "She's getting *paid* to say this?"

But I wasn't finished. "Be sure to clean the pickup truck," I told him. "And don't forget to open the door for her."

I gave him a blow-by-blow description of how to handle himself like a gentleman, and then, after I'd wished him luck, I said, "Call me back and let me know how it goes."

A week later the man called back. The date had been a great success, he said. They had gone to a movie and had had a wonderful time, and now they were going out on a *second* date.

After the second date he called back again. Things were going so well he had an even bigger problem.

"How do I kiss her?" he asked.

If there was ever going to be a test of my ability to communicate, this was it! How could I, nonvisually over the radio, tell a man how to kiss a girl? Now we're separating the good broadcasters from the bad!

By this time the man had begun to catch the fancy of the listening public. Right after his second date I had started getting letters from listeners who empathized with this lovelorn dairy farmer. What's more, people called in, wanting to find out how he was doing or offering up advice of their own. Men and women alike latched on to the idea of this simple, gentlehearted man who wanted nothing more than to meet a girl he could love. It was a poignant story of boy-meets-girl that touched the yearnings of hundreds of people, not for some jet-set romance but for sweet, innocent love.

So I told him how to kiss his girl. "Be sure to do it in the pickup," I said. "Sit close to her, and let your arm relax on the back of the car seat.

"And whatever you do, please shave!" I exhorted.

I told him every possible thing I could think of. "Gargle! Use deodorant!"

It may sound absurd in the retelling, but to me, at that moment, this call was the most important thing in the world. I felt it was critical to tell him *everything* I knew about kissing. This wasn't some frivolous question. It was this man's *life*, for goodness' sake.

Like all those listeners out there who were cheering him on, I wanted him to do it right. I didn't want him to blow it.

My advice must have worked.

Eight months and many phone calls on radio later, the dairy farmer proposed to the woman he met on that first date. She accepted, and they were married in a small church wedding not long after.

I was invited to the wedding, but in the end I decided not to go. Before the wedding I had talked to the bride-to-be on the air, and she had said discreetly, "We'd love you to come, but there are people who might know who you are."

I realized in a blinding flash that she was trying to tell me, "Don't come."

"Every bride deserves a day," I thought. And so I stayed away. But not long ago I called to see how they were doing.

They had a new cow—a black-and-white Holstein.

Her name: Sally Jessy! I have the picture of the cow on the piano along with photos of my family.

As I marvel at the way this dairy farmer's life turned out, I can only feel humbled that I was able to play a small role in making happiness happen for him.

But why would someone like this dairy farmer call a perfect stranger hundreds of miles away to ask her some of the most personal questions on his mind?

What happened in this case was that a man in a small town in Wisconsin, in the dark of night, suddenly realized that he had a secret source of information—a woman sitting far away in a radio studio in New York City. Thanks to his secret source, he could quietly go about changing his life without stirring up gossip. No one in town needed to know why he was dressing better, looking happier, and shining his pickup truck.

With me, a faraway friend who wouldn't laugh at his questions or push him aside because she was "too busy," his secret was safe.

That's why people call me. One seventy-two-year-old man called me for advice after his friends had told him he was a fool to think of getting married at his age. But he was no dirty old man lusting after some spring chicken. Instead, he was a southern gentleman yearning to recapture bygone joys in the winter of his life.

Years before, during World War II, he had parachuted into Norway, where he had met a girl who worked in a bakery shop. She befriended him, and before long he was spending time with her and her family.

When the war was over, he returned home to the South and made his fortune.

"God has been good to me," he told me. Southerners never tell you they're rich. They always put it euphemistically.

At any rate, although he was rich, the man never married. Often his mind would carry him back to Norway, to the young woman in the bakery shop.

Because he was a simple man with simple pleasures, he never thought of traveling to Europe. But when his battalion had a reunion not long ago, he returned to the town in Norway where he had landed many years before.

There, in the bakery shop, was his friend. By now she was a little old lady with gray hair pulled back in a bun. She, too, had never married, and the two picked up as if it were yesterday. The war years were as fresh in her memory as the bread she baked each day. In a drawer in the bakeshop she kept a memento given to her by his battalion.

Again they said good-bye, and he returned to the States. But this time his mind remained back in Norway with his newfound love.

"Am I crazy, or can I marry this lady?" the southern gentleman asked me. "My friends told me it was the stupidest idea they had ever heard—a man marrying at seventy-two for the first time."

"I think it's the *best* idea I ever heard," I told him. "Get on that plane right now."

A month later he called back to say he had done exactly what I told him. He married his Norwegian sweetheart and brought her back to the States. I even got to talk to her on the phone. She spoke mainly Norwegian, but I felt a kinship with the woman. Maybe that's because of Karl and his Norwegian forebears. I hope the southerner and his Scandinavian will live happily ever after.

Why did I tell him to "go for it"?

In this case I saw no earthly reason why this man should live out his days *alone* with his large wealth. It simply didn't make sense. How boring for him to be by himself when he could be experiencing the joy of sharing his life with someone else—especially when that "someone else" had been on his mind for forty years!

That man had a dream. My job was to encourage him to live out his dream and be all he could be.

The way I see things, it doesn't matter if you're a forty-one-year-old dairy farmer or a seventy-two-year-old millionaire. You still can have the thrill of living your life to the fullest. It's your life; run with it!

One of the things that shocks me to the core as I answer the phone night after night is that most people dream very small dreams. I'm appalled at the narrowness of people's visions for themselves. Some people will call up, and their problem is money and their dream is to get a ten-dollar raise. I think if money matters, you should be lying awake thinking about how to make a million. Others will call and dream of being a buyer in a department store. I say, Why not dream of *owning* the department store?

Since dreams are free, I see no reason for not dreaming the ultimate dreams for yourself. We've been taught that somehow it's wrong to have grandiose dreams. But to my way of thinking, big dreams are wonderful. In the first place, it's *fun* to fantasize. Also, dreaming stretches you to strive to be the very best you can.

But most people are afraid to think big. They're afraid that if they verbalize their innermost secrets and confess that they want to be President of the United States or chairman of the board of IBM, someone will laugh at them.

This is especially true of women. Many women dream small dreams, particularly when it comes to jobs. Women don't think in terms of making big money. Their role model is the lady down the street who's gotten her real estate license. That's the way the typical suburban housewife thinks. If one of her friends gets a small job to earn a few dollars, she'll try to get one, too. She does not watch somebody on television or a top executive in business and say, "That could be me." She tends to relate only to the goal of some friend.

Our attitudes toward work haven't changed for decades. Despite the hullabaloo made by the women's movement, I feel most women go out and work to earn dollars to help the family. Men go out and work for careers.

I hear this discrepancy on the radio night after night. Typically, men ask me sophisticated questions: "How do I write a good cover letter for my résumé?" and "I've been in the job two years, I've got a good offer from another firm, should I leave?" These are usually male questions.

Female questions are much more personality oriented. "There's a girl in my office who I think is reading my mail," someone says timidly. "What should I do about it?"

Instead of being aggressive and thinking about how they could move forward in their careers, many women simply wait and react to situations on the job.

Most women I talk to believe that a job should be reasonably feminine, not high-pressured or successful. Too much achievement would impinge on male prerogatives and may even threaten the men. Also, women often assume a job is temporary. Teenage girls tell me, "I'll work for a few years before I have my family." The trouble is, when she gets that family, she discovers too late that she's working through the baby, through the bringing up, through everything—with no career plan.

But women have got to stop thinking that they're going to be in the workplace part time. If you're going to spend the hours, you might as well make bucks—or at least reap some significant emotional rewards.

One of the reasons I'm so adamant on the issue of women and work is that the subject strikes a raw nerve with me personally. I witnessed firsthand my mother's financial helplessness through my father's declining years. As a young wife I felt the humiliation of having to be dependent on my first husband's largess for money to help my parents. Once, when I asked him if his well-to-do parents could give me a two-thousand-dollar loan to pay some medical bills for my father, they sent him a letter with this brutal reply: "Her father's a loser. The money will never be paid back. As your financial advisers and parents, we recommend that you don't extend a loan to him."

That signaled the end of my first marriage and the beginning of my determination to control my own life through an independent career. I started to think, "If I'd had the money, I wouldn't have had to ask them for two thousand dollars." From that moment on I was transformed from a person who was never conscious of being a financial success herself to someone who wanted to have enough money of her own to be free of dependency. That set a tone for the relationship I have with Karl and for my unswerving belief that you should never be financially at anybody's disposal—even somebody you love.

So that's why night after night I exhort women and men alike to take charge of their lives and start dreaming big dreams. That advice is not just pie-in-the-sky idealism. It's rooted in hard-nosed practicality born of my own life experience.

Another thing that guides my thoughts as I give advice over the radio is a desire to build self-esteem in my listeners. I find that there is an epidemic lack of self-esteem in this country that is growing by leaps and bounds.

Americans suffer from a giant inferiority complex. Furthermore, we are communicating this sense of inferiority to our children. The average child hears ten "nos" to every one "yes." We don't give our kids a belief that they are important as individuals and that there is a place in this world for them. As a result, we have a nation of adults and youngsters who are driven by the need to belong because they haven't got the inner strength to succeed on their own: I must go steady in third grade; I must find a new husband; I must get pregnant in order to be somebody; I must get remarried or I'll be a nobody.

The feeling of inferiority infects every aspect of our lives.

This national crisis of self-esteem was brought home to me a few years ago on a trip to Italy, where I was the guest of Giuliana di Camerino. She's the female fashion mogul who owns the Roberta di Camerino boutiques located on all the classiest avenues in the world.

Giuliana's own story is the story of a woman who believed in herself, despite the odds. Her saga always reminds me of the movie *The Garden of the Finzi-Continis,* which chronicled an Italian-Jewish family in World War II. During the war, Giuliana's wealthy family lost everything and escaped to Switzerland. There, she got a job in a handbag factory and learned the trade that eventually became the foundation of her fortune.

After the war, Giuliana returned to Italy and opened her own handbag company in Venice. She named the company "Roberta" after the 1933 musical comedy starring Fred Astaire and Ginger Rogers. That bit of whimsy was the beginning of her fashion empire.

Giuliana and I had first met in America through a mutual friend who told her I was very good at giving romantic advice. In this wonderful Italian way she immediately embraced me into her life with an ebullient *"Ciao, bambina."* Then she proceeded to discuss her romantic problems.

Since romantic liaisons are on the order of major-league baseball in Italy, her love life was a little more exalted and complicated than that of the average Wisconsin dairy farmer. But love is love, and I tried to give her some advice.

In return, she invited me to a lavish party in her wonderful palazzo on the Grand Canal in Venice. It was a delightful party, but what was especially exciting about it was the mix of people. There were eighty-year-olds and there were sixteen-year-olds, and nobody seemed very worried about age. They were totally comfortable with each other and with who they were.

It didn't hurt *my* self-esteem, of course, to be asked out by two gentlemen: one my age and one eighteen years old! Although I declined their offers, I thought it was wonderful that people could be so free. It was okay for a married lady like me to flirt a little with an eighteen-year-old and not feel that it meant something significant.

What was even more impressive about the Italians was their sense of self-worth. When I went with Giuliana to a small village where she had some business, she proudly introduced me to some of the townspeople. One of them was the village trashman, who was going around picking up refuse. Another was the postal clerk, who welcomed me warmly and eagerly told me about his job and showed me around the post office.

Remarkably, everybody in this town felt good about himself. You didn't hear people in this small town sitting around agonizing over their self-esteem. These were Italians who didn't have to look for self-worth. They seemed to be born with it. Their physical bearing fairly shouted: "Here I am. I'm Giovanni, and I do *this!*"

Whether it was Giuliana, the millionaire fashion empress, Antonio, the garbageman, or Giuseppe, the postman, everyone had an essential respect for every other person and for himself.

Everywhere I traveled during the next couple of years, I asked questions to see how people really felt about themselves.

Do the English have a problem with self-esteem? By and large, the answer was no.

Do the French? The French! Sometimes they think they're God's gift to the world.

Do you see the Germans agonizing over whether or not they're somebody, or the Israelis or the Chinese? No.

Ours is one of the few countries in the world where what you *do* seems to be a mark of who you *are*.

Back home in America, all I get are calls from people who feel *awful* about themselves. The underlying message that comes through is that somehow we have failed to communicate to our children the *realistic* sense of possibilities that life holds. One of the culprits is the mass media, which holds up idealized and unrealistic role models.

That's why I feel an almost missionary zeal about encouraging people to be all they can be. I never bludgeon people with my advice. But I do try to help people draw out decisions that enable them to take action.

Sometimes, though, I have to hold myself back from giving advice—even when I'm certain it's good—because I sense that the callers need to find some things out for themselves. That's especially true for adopted children who are seeking their identities as they search for their natural parents.

After all these years as J.J.'s adoptive parent, it pains me terribly to get calls from people who are searching for their "real" parents. I get those kinds of calls four and five times a night. Somehow these individuals want to discover their heredities, their original parents, their birthrights, as if that knowledge would make them secure and confident. In their singlemindedness, they forget that their adoptive parents can't help but feel rejected.

I don't put much stock in those searches. It may be very American, but I cannot believe that you are simply the blood you are born to. The way you arrive in this world is that a man gets in bed with a woman and a sperm passes in the night. That's it. Yet that sperm, which you can buy in a clinic, has nothing to do with parenting.

A parent is the person who takes you home from a

hospital, pays your bills, stays up all night with you when you're sick, cares about your future, educates you, and teaches you. A parent has nothing to do with sperm.

The bottom line is that parenting is not birthing. Birthing is birthing, and parenting is something else altogether.

Ninety-nine percent of the time, when an adopted child does find what he's looking for, the natural parents turn out to be a disappointment. Occasionally someone will call me and say, "I found my father, and he's terrific!"

But is he a prince? Is he the heir to a throne? Is he filthy rich and going to leave you all his money? Are your expectations realistic?

Of course not.

Do I convey these hard, cold facts to the caller searching for his parent? Not always, because I can tell from the sound of his voice that he wants so desperately to continue his search in order to find a magical solution to his problems.

There are some callers, however, whose voices betray an urgency that demands an immediate and decisive response. That was the case with a woman who called one night distraught because her husband had walked out, leaving her with four small children to care for.

After we had talked for five minutes or so about how she should proceed with her life, it became obvious to me that her life might not proceed very much further. Her speech was starting to slur, and even though she never said anything about taking her own life, I knew immediately that she was in deep trouble.

I signaled to the producer to cut all the commercials so I could keep talking to her. I knew enough about suicide calls to hold her on the line as long as I could. While I was on the phone with her, the producer was busy trying to locate her address. Every call that comes in to me is first screened by a producer, who gets some facts about the caller. So even though I don't ask for that information over the air, many times we could find someone if we had to.

The producer traced the woman's address and sent an emergency squad to her home.

It arrived just in time. She had taken an overdose of sleeping pills, and if I hadn't kept her awake and talking on the line, the squad said, she might have died.

I heard from the woman again several months later. She was doing fine and was managing to hold her family together without her husband.

In all the years I've been giving advice on radio, few calls leave me speechless. But one night the producer, Nancy, had a call on hold and warned me during a commercial break, "This is going to be a weird one."

"What is it?" I asked.

"Some guy who's got the best Bob Hope imitation I ever heard."

"Sounds like fun," I said. "Put him on."

A man came on the line and said, "Hi, Sally. This is Bob. Everything is fine here in Hollywood. I'm calling to ask for advice because it's Christmastime and I have to work. I'm feeling sorry for myself because all my friends are going to Palm Springs and I can't go because I have to work on my TV special."

For a few seconds my mind went blank, and I didn't know quite how to respond. I was about to pipe in and tell him it was the best imitation I had ever heard when something inside stopped me short. This imitation was too *good*. There aren't a lot of people in this business— Rich Little maybe—who could do such a convincing routine.

So I played it straight. "Bob, let me help you with your problem," I said. We chatted for a few minutes, he plugged his Christmas special, and then he signed off.

A week or so later one of our public relations people gave me a call. "Bob Hope gave me a ring and wanted me to thank you. He loved talking to you because you didn't ask, 'Are you really Bob Hope?' "

Like everybody else in America, even Bob Hope, it seems, sometimes needs a friend who will take him seriously!

If you think all this talking on the air was falling on deaf ears, you're wrong. I had been busy listening to other people's problems night after night and giving my best advice to satisfy the desires of their hearts. But it also turns out that someone out there was listening to *my* unspoken desires.

One day back in 1983 a special man and his wife were on vacation in Mexico and happened to be flicking their radio dial when they picked up my show on Talknet out of Albuquerque. There must have been something about the sound of my voice that captured his imagination. As soon as he got home from vacation, he mentioned my name to one of the executives at the broadcasting conglomerate he worked for.

"There's a woman on radio you should check into," the man said. "Maybe she'd be good for Multimedia."

The man was Phil Donahue. In a strange twist of fate it was Phil, now my fellow talk show host, who paved the way for my great leap forward into TV talk.

CHAPTER ELEVEN

Howdy Doody's Descendant

ACTUALLY IT WASN'T PHIL DONAHUE but Howdy Doody who played the most decisive role in starting me on the road to my syndicated TV talk show.

Burt Dubrow, a former member of the peanut gallery on the *Howdy Doody* show, was producing a TV interview show for Multimedia Entertainment out of Cincinnati. When a colleague suggested he try me out as a guest on his show, he wasn't exactly overwhelmed.

"Who the heck is Sally Jessy Raphaël?" he said. Actually he said something considerably stronger, but it's not the kind of thing Howdy Doody would want repeated.

Burt was one of those people who, like me, was hooked on broadcasting from an early age. In his case it was television. He spent hours and hours in front of the set, watching anyone who was on: Uncle Miltie; Ed Sullivan; Lucille Ball. When he was ten, he got himself a ventriloquist's dummy and did birthday parties and magic shows to entertain neighborhood kids.

He also displayed the kind of trait that later made him a good producer: He was a persistent, noodgy kid, who would badger his favorite TV personalities until they agreed to meet him.

One of these was "Officer Joe Bolton," a favorite kiddy personality in the fifties on WPIX in New York. Burt wrote him so many letters that Officer Joe finally gave in. "Would you please come to the show? I *must* meet you," he wrote back.

Burt also had one of those lucky accidents of birth. He grew up down the street from Buffalo Bob Smith, the beloved foil of everybody's favorite wooden head, Howdy Doody. Naturally, with a neighbor like Buffalo Bob, Burt got to be in the peanut gallery more than a dozen times.

The peanut gallery was such a formative experience for Burt that he later dropped out of college to become the emcee and road manager for Buffalo Bob's *Howdy Doody Revival,* which toured the country back in the early seventies. To this day he and Buffalo Bob are still such fast friends that they talk on the phone at least three times a week.

Burt went on to become one of the producers for *The Mike Douglas Show* and ABC's *Kids Are People Too,* and eventually he found his way to Multimedia. The company sent him to Cincinnati to produce *Braun and Company,* a popular interview program in the area. That's what he was doing when his colleague suggested he book me as a guest.

Reluctantly Burt agreed. He still didn't have any idea who I was or why I should be on. To test the waters, he included my name in an announcement of upcoming guests a week before the show. Immediately the phones started ringing from my radio fans asking when I was slated to appear.

But even that didn't sway Burt. He figured I had rounded up all my friends and told them to call the station!

As for me, I wasn't giving much thought to my appearance on this local TV show. To me it was just another opportunity to plug my radio program. So I flew to Cincinnati, did *Braun and Company,* flew back to New York, and promptly forgot the whole thing.

A few weeks later Burt called back.

"We want you to be on the show again, *not* because you're a good guest—which you weren't—but because you have a large following," said Burt. He was facing a ratings period, he said, and he wanted someone who could pull in viewers.

I couldn't believe this guy was talking to me this way. I mean, *nobody* says things like that to your face.

Instead of being insulted, I was amused by this brash young man who had just dressed me down and built me up at the same time. So I decided to go back.

Before the show Burt sat me down and said bluntly, "Look, the last time you were really lousy. You were too timid." I made some excuse about holding back because I didn't want to take over the show, but he didn't let me off the hook.

"Don't you worry about that," he said. "Just be who you are."

My second time as a guest I was more assertive. This time Burt approved. "You were better," he said. "How about filling in as host for one week?"

His offer came out of nowhere, and I wasn't prepared. Nor was I prepared for the emotions that surged through me as I contemplated doing TV again. Some of my previous experiences with television had been terrible. In Miami they forced me to talk to the water commissioner; in New York they wanted me to change my looks every day. What was going to happen to me this time?

But no matter how afraid I was of being beaten down again, I knew I had to confront the fear head-on. That's what I had done all my life, and I couldn't stop now. I may have had doubts about doing television, but there was something I loved even more: I absolutely *loved* the challenge. I was my father's daughter, after all, and I could never turn away from a risk.

So I took up Burt's challenge. For several days before the show Burt and I brainstormed about the approach I should take on the air. I told him I was best when I related to the audience the way I did on radio. It had to be person to person, or it wouldn't be me.

"You want to be Mr. Rogers for adults, right?" said Burt.

That said it all. I would talk directly to the audience at home, not just to the guests. That way the viewers would be drawn into the show as participants.

I went on the air in Cincinnati for a week, and before long Burt was talking about bigger things. It seems that he had a development deal with Multimedia that gave him the green light to create a brand-new show. What he had in mind, he said, was a talk show with a woman as host. At the time there was no woman on TV doing a show of any substance without a man sitting next to her as "cohost."

What's more, he wanted to capitalize on a new trend. The woman over forty was starting to look good to the TV moguls. All of a sudden it was not an embarrassment to be over forty in television, and now Burt wanted someone who could fill the bill.

That's where I came in.

"Would you be interested in having a show of your own?" he asked me one day during my week hosting *Braun and Company*.

"Sure, sure," I said offhandedly. Inside I was numb. I had heard this kind of question so many times in my career, and so many times it had gone nowhere.

But the very next day he introduced me to the chief executive officer of Multimedia, a wonderful bear of a man named Walter Bartlett. Walter was simple and direct and genuinely seemed to want to know how I reacted to the idea of doing my own show.

I can remember thinking, "What a lovely guy. Wouldn't it be fun to work for him?" We shook hands, and although I wasn't sure what was coming next, I felt really good about meeting him.

Before I knew it, I was signing a proposal for a television show, and Multimedia was giving me some money so I wouldn't sign with anybody else.

"That's nice," I thought. "I'll just take the money, which wasn't much anyway, they'll bury the project, and I won't have to worry about it anymore."

But they didn't bury the project. A few weeks later Burt called me in New York to say that he was moving ahead with the deal. We'd do a pilot, he said, and then we'd start taping the show—from St. Louis, Missouri.

"Wait a minute!" I said to Karl. "What are we getting ourselves into?" Here I thought it was just "take the money and run." But they were really going to do this. So now what should I do? Walter Bartlett really meant what he said. He was an honest man. And now they were going to do the show and they were going to do it in *St. Louis!*

Holy mackerel! What was going to happen to my radio work? What was going to happen to my kids? I'd better think about this *seriously.*

Before I threw myself into this show, I wanted to know exactly what the stakes were. I went to everyone I knew in show business asking for advice, and everywhere the advice was the same: "This is just a local show, like a million local television shows everywhere. It's going to go nowhere. It's only a matter of weeks before it dies."

It was clear the odds were stacked against me. If two thousand pilots are done every year, maybe two get put on the air, and one of *those* is canceled. Those looked worse than casino odds to me. They were lottery odds. Of course, this couldn't work. How could a low-budget show in St. Louis ever hope to go national?

Then there was the thorny problem of Burt. The guy might pick up and move to St. Louis. I mean, he was putting his whole life on the line for this show. He was committing himself to it.

It was bad enough that Burt was going to St. Louis. But I still had a job on radio with Talknet out of New York, and now it looked as if I had to *commute* to St. Louis. I was going to kill myself. My friends promised that this would last only a couple of weeks. So maybe I could commute for a couple of months, but then what?

I didn't have time to think about what was coming next. I had a show to do in St. Louis.

At first we called the program *In Touch with Sally Jessy Raphaël*. There was a theme, a guest or series of guests, and a studio audience that I could interact with.

A week went by, and I was still doing it. Several months went by, and the show continued to go on. A year passed, and *still* I was doing the show. The problem was, even after a year the show was being carried only by the station in St. Louis. I was sure this meant my days were numbered, and I was beginning to wait for the ax to fall.

"Any minute now these people are going to pull the plug," I thought.

How could they *not* pull the plug? Everything about the show seemed to be wrong, starting with me. My clothes were wrong: I wore pants, and everybody hated them. I gained weight; then I lost weight. If there was a snowstorm, some days we had five people turn up for the audience. I can remember one show on evangelism where we had six people onstage and five people in the audience!

I was so sure the show was a goner that I called all my friends in New York. "The end is near," I said.

Just as I was sure I was about to get canned in walked Walter Bartlett with a big smile on his face. He put his arm around me and said, "Sally, I don't want you to worry about a thing. You're doing just fine. We're behind you a hundred percent."

In that moment all my preconceptions about the way broadcasting works disappeared. It may sound corny, but at last here was a company that *cared*. In Walter Bartlett I had someone who was willing to go the distance with me. He was ready to back me up 100 percent until I made it. That's what Multimedia had done for Phil Donahue, through his early years in Dayton. It took the long view and stuck with him until he became a star. Now it looked as if it was doing it for me.

I was so dumbfounded I couldn't think straight. "What's happening here?" I wondered.

What was happening was that little by little I was being groomed for success. I was Howdy Doody, and Burt Dubrow was pulling the strings. Everything he thought he would do with Howdy, he did with me.

The truth is that the person you see in front of the camera today on *Sally Jessy Raphaël* is a gentler person than she was when the show started in St. Louis back in 1983. Some of my moves, my clothes, and my energy level were restyled to project a positive image for television.

I may have been a natural for radio, but on television my style came across as abrasive. As a host I was too opinionated, too quick to interrupt the guests with my advice. Most people were watching the show because they wanted to find out what the guests had to say. In the beginning we didn't even need guests. I had so much to say that I could have sat in both chairs!

On radio I was a friendly voice of authority. On TV I sounded too strong. And strong doesn't sell, at least not for long. It may work for a while for some men, like Morton Downey, Jr. But over the long haul the hosts with the greatest staying power on television have been people who are comfortable to watch. People like Garry Moore, Arthur Godfrey, Mike Douglas, Dinah Shore, and Virginia Graham all are *nice* people, who are easy to have in your home day after day.

So I had to learn to tone down my voice and my opinions if I wanted to make it on television. I had to come across as warm, comfortable, and feminine, the kind of friend you'd like to chat with over coffee.

But it wasn't only my interviewing style that didn't go over. As I said, my clothes, too, worked against me. I wore pants every day because that's all I owned. The viewers hated them. They wrote letters criticizing my wardrobe and choice of colors. Burt got rid of the pants and put me in skirts.

"You're a role model, Sally," he said. "You've gotta look terrific. You've gotta look feminine; you've gotta look soft."

If you think I went along with all these changes without putting up a fight, you're wrong. Week after week I slugged it out with Burt on every change he wanted to make.

Sometimes, just to tweak him, I'd show up in an elegant dress and sneakers. I get terribly restrained by the need to dress "correctly." The Sally who appears on television is in many ways so alien to my nature. My nature is to be expressive with clothing—to use it in a theatrical way as a costume. I like to change constantly, to experiment with my clothes, my makeup, and my hair.

I'm really a nine-year-old inside, and like all nine-year-olds, when the pressures to conform are more than I can bear, I have to rebel or I go nuts.

That's why I showed up at work one day with my hair spiked like a punk rocker. At the time Karl and I were about to go on vacation, and I decided to trick the staff and have my hair done a few days early. If I had sneaked in wearing an odd piece of clothing, they would have caught me and re-dressed me. But they couldn't paste my hair back on!

I walked into the studio, and Burt screamed, "I'm gonna die! Why did you do that, Sally? You still have five shows to tape."

I just shrugged. My life is so disciplined that often it feels good to be a bit bad. Since my hair was all chopped up and spiked, there wasn't much anyone could do to change it, so I did the shows anyway.

In the end, though, I settled down and went along with Burt's direction. It wasn't that I agreed with him. But deep down I trusted him. I trusted him most of all, I suppose, because from the very beginning he had believed in me.

That's the one thing you need in broadcasting, and it's so rare. I secretly believe that there are more villains than good guys in this business. Burt is a good guy. He should wear white.

His response to my red eyeglasses symbolized that trust. Those glasses were *me*. They were my little rebellion against tradition, a visual message that hinted at the fiery sparks of drama in my inner personality.

Some powers that be at Multimedia took one look at those big red glasses and insisted that I trade them in for a more conservative pair.

But Burt is a masterful politician, and immediately he dreamed up a foolproof scheme to keep me seeing red.

"Tell Karl to buy five of the ugliest pairs of glasses he can find," said Burt.

Karl found them, and Burt rolled into action. He made a tape of me interviewing guests wearing each of my ugly new spectacles. Last of all came the red ones.

Then he marched in to see the top executives of the company and showed them the tape. One by one each pair of glasses was rejected. Finally they saw the light.

"You know, she's right," the executives said in agreement. "The red ones do look best!"

With my trademark red glasses intact, I listened and learned from Burt. Under his tutelage I grew, and the show gradually started gaining momentum. Before long we weren't just in St. Louis but in dozens of cities across the country.

The stories we did every day weren't the front-page kinds of issues that Phil Donahue does so well, but intensely personal stories, of ordinary people caught in extraordinary circumstances of danger or tragedy or crisis.

One of these people was a young woman named Stephie who was burning to reveal a secret—a secret so personal that she had kept it from her parents, from her friends, and even from her husband.

Stephie had been laid off from her job as manager of a turnpike Howard Johnson's in Connecticut. To keep herself company while she puttered around the house, she turned on the TV every morning. She'd watch Phil Donahue, and then, since *Sally Jessy Raphaël* followed, she stayed tuned.

Day after day, as she watched my show, she became convinced that she should share her secret with me. When I mentioned on TV that I did a radio show at night, a plan formulated in her mind. She would tell everything to me—not face-to-face—but on radio.

Stephie reasoned that if she got her secret out in the open, if she said it out loud to someone who would understand, maybe her nightmares would stop.

One night she got up her nerve and called me on radio. She waited on the line until the producers put her call through. But when she heard me say, "Hi, I'm Sally Jessy Raphaël," Stephie froze. She hung up. A few days later she called again. And again she hung up. A third time she called, and this time she poured out her story in a torrent of words and emotions.

"I was raped when I was fifteen," Stephie said. "I was on a date, and he raped me, and I was so scared and ashamed I never told anyone. This happened fourteen years ago, but now I feel like I'm going crazy. What's happening to me?" Her voice was quivering as the words tumbled out, yet she pushed on until she had told the story in every detail.

I'm not even sure what I said to her at the time; but we talked for a while, and then she said good-bye.

Several months later at the TV studio we came across a letter from Stephie in a pile of viewer mail. It wasn't the first letter she had written to me, but somehow the others had gotten lost. She wanted to talk again, she said, and I was the only person she felt comfortable talking to.

Immediately we put one of our top producers, Terry Murphy, on Stephie's case. Terry tried to convince her to fly to St. Louis and appear on television, but Stephie was too embarrassed. Before long, though, she was telling her story to Terry. From then on the two talked regularly over the phone, and after a few weeks Stephie agreed to come on the show.

Alone and scared, Stephie flew to St. Louis. She had never been on an airplane in her life, yet she bravely took the trip and checked into the Clarion Hotel, which was also where Karl and I had our suite. When she arrived and discovered that Terry would not be able to be with her in the studio the next day because of a family emergency, she panicked. Terry had become her lifeline, her protector and friend. And now she was completely alone.

Once again I was the only one she could turn to. And we had never met face-to-face.

I heard a knock at my door, and when I opened it, there in front of me was Stephie, pale and frightened in an old T-shirt and jeans. Her cheeks were streaked with tears, and her eyes were swollen from hours of crying.

I immediately ushered her into the room, where I was in the midst of broadcasting my radio show. Stephie sat and listened to the show, and afterward I tried to get her to talk about her feelings.

She was still so scared she wouldn't open her mouth.

If she couldn't talk in the hotel, I thought, how was she going to open up the next day on television?

For the next few hours I did my best to prepare her for the TV show. Professionally I knew that if Stephie backed out, the show would be weaker without her testimony. We had other guests scheduled to appear, but they all were "experts."

More important than the media considerations, though, was Stephie herself. "I've got to be honest with you," I said. "Whatever you say on television tomorrow will be heard all over the country. Are you ready for that?"

I did such a good job of talking her out of appearing that she was pretty much ready to back out. But I sensed that she really wanted to speak out about what had happened to her. Obviously it had helped her to tell me about the rape over the radio. But something must not have been settled in her mind, or she wouldn't have persisted in writing me letters or flown all the way to St. Louis to talk to me. We talked on into the night, and by the time she left, Stephie was ready to go on the show.

She did appear, and she was wonderful. Quietly and methodically, she told her story in every heart-wrenching detail.

"When I was fifteen, I was visiting relatives, and I went out with some friends," Stephie said. "My date was an eighteen-year-old guy who was a friend of a friend. There were five or six of us, and we were driving around and drinking and stuff.

"Then, about two in the morning, they pulled the car over, and we got out and walked in the woods. I guess I should have gotten suspicious then, but I didn't think too much about it at first. But when my date and I got ahead of the other kids, I started to get a little concerned.

"He claimed he wanted to show me a haunted house, and we walked through this park up on a mountain where you could see the whole city.

"As beautiful as it was, I was getting really scared. We were all alone up there on this mountain, and there was no haunted house in sight.

"I wanted to go back. It was getting late, and by now I could sense that something was wrong.

" 'Come a little further,' he said.

"I got scared. We were holding hands, and he was walking faster and faster.

"I pulled back on his hand and said, 'Let's go home.'

"That's when it happened. He jerked me down to the

muddy ground, sat on top of me, and raped me. I tried to scream, but I couldn't. His hands were around my neck choking me so hard that I couldn't even make a sound.

"I could hear my friends only a few yards away calling, 'Stephie, Stephie.' But it didn't do any good. His fingers tightened on my neck so hard I could barely breathe.

"After the sounds of the people moved away, he got up and said with a sneer, 'If you ever tell anyone, I swear to God I'll *kill* you.'

"That was the last thing I remembered. I must have passed out because the next thing I knew, I was in a car with my friends. Two hours had passed. I don't remember them finding me, and I don't remember them bringing me to the car. I just remember going to a friend's house and taking a shower and changing clothes. I didn't want to go to the hospital. If I did, my father might find out, and I was scared to death of what he might do to me. He was from the old country, and he would never have understood."

The next day, Stephie said, she saw her friends again, and they all acted as if nothing had happened.

Stephie acted as if nothing had happened, too. But in truth, the rape drove her to despair. She began to drink. She even kept liquor in her locker in high school and would sneak drinks between classes.

Even worse, soon after the rape she became pregnant by the rapist. She thought there was only one thing she could do: She had to have an abortion. But she couldn't tell her parents, and she had no money to pay for it. In desperation she was forced to lie to the one person she loved the most—her boyfriend—who is now her husband.

"I told him it was his baby so that he'd pay for it," she confessed to the TV audience.

Stephie went ahead and had the abortion, she said, but she felt such remorse that she vowed she would punish herself forever. She was standing in church at the baptism of her infant niece, who was the very age her aborted child would have been, when an overwhelming feeling of shame flooded over her. As she held her niece in her arms, Stephie promised God, "I'll never, ever have kids."

But that wasn't the end of Stephie's ordeal. The rape, the abortion, the self-loathing, and the fear drove her to attempt suicide. A friend got her to a hospital, and it was then that Stephie had to make a choice.

"I either had to be hospitalized or go to Alcoholics Anonymous," she said.

She went to AA. Eventually she married her high school sweetheart and became manager of a restaurant. That was what she had been doing for ten years before she called me on the radio.

But even though her life moved on, the rape was still with her. She was haunted by nightmares. In her dreams, she said, she saw her rapist standing over her menacingly, saying, "I'll kill you if you speak out."

It wasn't until she was laid off from her job, though, that she knew the time had come for her to speak out.

"Everything I watched on TV, in magazines, and in the movies seemed to be about rape. It was almost as though someone were pushing it on me—pushing me toward my decision to speak out.

"That's why I'm here now," she told the audience.

When Stephie finished telling her story on the air, the audience was overcome with emotion.

I was filled with pride. "You did it. It's all over," I said to her.

With that the audience broke into electric applause.

Stephie couldn't move. She was virtually glued to her seat, and we had to get one of our producers to pick her up off the chair and carry her off the set.

It would be nice to be able to say that by speaking out on my show, Stephie was cured of her nightmares and lived happily ever after. All that did happen, but not exactly for the reasons you might think.

At first Stephie's nightmares grew worse. After she left St. Louis, Stephie became terribly frightened that her rapist would see the show and come back and kill her. A recurrent dream plagued her. In the dream she saw herself in a church with four coffins. Three of them were filled. One of them was open and empty. "Who is that for?" she asked a priest. But she knew the answer. It was for her.

As for me, I couldn't get her out of my mind. I had a nagging sense that I should *do* something to help her. In those hours in the hotel room I had become her confidante and friend. Somehow I had to do more. But I had no idea how to go about it.

What happened next is the stuff of miracles.

The day the Stephie show was broadcast, something occurred that almost never takes place in television. There was a freak transmission, and my show was broadcast by accident in Rocky Mount, Virginia, on a channel that usually came in as static.

As a result, a human behavior counselor named Sandy Meyer, who had been sexually abused herself as a child, inadvertently became a viewer that day. Sandy had never seen my program before—and she probably never saw it again after that accidental broadcast occurred. But when she heard Stephie's story, she said to herself, "I can help that person."

Immediately, she picked up the phone to call the television station that had broadcast my show. It turned out that the nearest station that carried the program was hundreds of miles away in North Carolina.

Sandy managed to track us down in St. Louis, and offered to give Stephie free counseling at the Sandy Meyer Center in Rocky Mount.

Once I got wind of her offer, I marched right in to Burt Dubrow's office. He could tell by the look on my face that I was up to something.

"Don't ask me for anything," he said.

"Burt, this woman will treat Stephie for free, and I want us to pick up the cost of her trip."

"This is absolutely great," he said, unconvinced. "We are turning this TV show into a social service agency."

In the end Burt relented. How could Howdy Doody say no when we were dealing with something on the order of an act of God? The fact that Stephie's letters had reached us and that she had appeared on the show was in itself a miracle. And then there was the matter of the "freak" transmission.

Stephie flew to Rocky Mount and went through a week of one-on-one therapy with Sandy Meyer. Three days into her therapy Stephie's nightmares disappeared.

A few weeks later, when Stephie told me about her transformation, I insisted that she fly to St. Louis again with Sandy Meyer to appear on the show a second time. When I saw her face-to-face, I knew that a miracle had indeed taken place.

I had never seen such a change in anyone in my life. She was smiling, confident, and proud, not at all like the shy, scared young woman I had met in my hotel room. Other people saw the change, too. Her husband, she said, had been crazy with joy ever since she had gotten back from Virginia. Even her landlady said she looked different. There was a gleam in her eye that fairly danced with delight.

A few weeks after she went back home, Stephie called with even more exciting news: She was pregnant! What's more, she had been pregnant when she appeared on my show the second time and hadn't known it.

What she had denied herself all those years had finally come to pass. She gave birth to a strapping baby boy, Aarty, named after her wonderful, patient husband, who's the salt of the earth.

And she promptly named *me* the godmother.

What that meant was that I had to go do my godmother thing at a Ukrainian church in Connecticut. My staff thought I was nuts to take time out from our already frantic schedule to go to a baptism, but there was no way I was going to miss this one. Stephie and I had become so close that she was part of my family.

What Karl and I hadn't quite bargained for, though, was that a baptism in a Ukrainian church is a heck of an ordeal. We just about passed out from the honor.

These days Stephie is like a sister to me. When we moved the production of the show from St. Louis to New Haven in 1987, she started dropping by the office every couple of weeks to let me see the baby. She and little Aarty sat in my dressing room while I put on makeup and had my hair fixed.

I'm crazy about Aarty. Since I don't have any grandchildren of my own, he's my chance to be off and running in the grandparent stakes.

Our lives are intertwined in other ways, too. Stephie is now a volunteer counselor at the New Haven Rape Crisis Center, and I've done my part as a guest speaker at one of its fund-raising events.

Obviously my relationship with Stephie goes way beyond the ties I develop with most of my guests. But her story goes to the heart of what I'm all about. I genuinely love meeting people like Stephie, and I relate to their pain.

Maybe the reason is that like them, I'm a survivor.

CHAPTER TWELVE

Meet Me in St. Louis

To UNDERSTAND the price you pay for success in television, you have to know what it was like to commute between New York and St. Louis every week for four years. From 1983, when we began in St. Louis, until 1987, when we moved the production of *Sally Jessy Raphaël* to New Haven, I was constantly on the run.

A more reasonable approach, of course, would have been to pack up the family and move to St. Louis. But my radio contract with NBC required that I broadcast live from New York three nights a week. So in order to fulfill the radio contract *and* tape the TV show in St. Louis three days a week, I had to do the seemingly impossible.

Ours was truly a fly-by-night schedule. On Sunday night Karl and I flew to St. Louis and checked into a hotel, where we lived until Wednesday. On Monday and Tuesday we taped several programs for TV, grabbed a bite to eat, and then broadcast the radio show from a special hookup in our hotel room. Originally we even had to drive to a radio station fifteen miles away to do the show, but mercifully that only lasted for two years.

On Wednesday we'd do our final TV tapings in St. Louis and then fly back to New York in time to go live on radio at night at the NBC studios in Rockefeller Center.

Thursday and Friday we broadcast again from the NBC studios.

From the beginning, of course, I thought the TV show was only a trial balloon and our zany schedule would only be temporary. So I kept telling the kids, "Mom will be gone a week or two." But a week turned into a month, and a month turned into a year, and a year turned into four years.

I actually spent *four years* commuting to St. Louis and telling my children that I'd be home any moment! For four years they were growing up like crazy. When I started commuting, J.J. was eleven. When I finally came back for good, he was fifteen. That's a big chunk of a boy's life.

The downside of all this is that for all those years, several days a week, J.J. was a latchkey kid. He wasn't completely alone, however. His two older sisters took turns looking after him. Every time there was an emergency, though, I'd have to handle it by phone from St. Louis. I was burning up the telephone wires, certain that he was going to become a juvenile delinquent.

He was a good kid, though, who never did anything worse than play on my guilt. "All the other kids have somebody to help with algebra—and you're not here!" he'd complain on the days when we were out of town.

But when we saw him again at the end of the week, our family life picked up where it had left off—in its normal state of frenzy and fun.

The stability of our family wasn't the only thing we sacrificed during our years of commuting. Our preoccupation with airline schedules finally dealt a deathblow to our restaurant.

One night in the dead of winter in 1983 we shut down the Wine Press for good. The wolf was at our door in the form of Uncle Sam, who was dunning us for back taxes. Restaurants are taxed for endless numbers of things: alcohol; withholding; doing business. Even without the taxes the cost of running the restaurant was milking us dry. Finally the writing appeared on the wall. Karl owed the government so much money that he couldn't afford to keep the place going.

So one night, at three o'clock in the morning, we closed the place down. We smeared some white paint over the name on the awning, and for a few minutes we sat in the restaurant with the lights out and tried to deal with our pain. For nearly four years, 365 nights a year, we had put our hearts into this place. Now our backs were up against the wall.

I packed up my little eggbeater collection and one of my mother's paintings, and we locked the door for good.

It was the biggest heartbreak Karl ever had. He had failed. And he had failed big. The owners of the building came after him for the rest of the money on the lease. Then the government came after Karl. In fact, one of the tragedies of our life is that he now owes so much money in restaurant taxes that he will probably spend the rest of his life paying it all back. Even more tragic to us is that we lost our friends' money.

In the big scheme of things any restaurant that remains in business for four years in New York City can be considered a success. Most go under in a year. Those are the statistics. But now you know the realities and the heartbreak behind the numbers. For us the restaurant was nothing short of disaster. Even now, whenever I hear the name Wine Press, my heart clutches.

Despite the restaurant debacle, all was not gloom and doom in the Soderlund household. When one door closes in our lives, another always seems to open. Usually it's the door to our apartment! The one thing that remained constant during this topsy-turvy period of our lives was our willingness to throw out the welcome mat to the world's "homeless." Any friend near or far who had a child who needed caring for, we obliged.

* * *

One night, very late, we were awakened by a telephone call. The connection was very squeaky and funny, and it sounded as if it might be coming from abroad.

"Hello, Sally. It's Norah." My brain raced through its computer to figure out who the heck Norah was. Then I remembered Darragh Owens's mother. In the eleven years since teenaged Darragh had left Florida and returned to Ireland, I hadn't really thought much about the Owens family.

But Norah plunged ahead as if I had spoken to her the day before.

"Sally, my little daughter, Catherine, is coming out to America. She wants to do some art thing."

Then her voice broke, and she was drowned out by a rash of static. A few moments later the voice was back.

"Would you please be looking after her?" Before I had a chance to say anything, we were drowned out again by the static. The last thing I heard was Norah screaming over the line the name of the airline and the time of her daughter's arrival at Kennedy Airport.

The next morning I thought I had dreamed it. But next to my bed were some notes I had scribbled about the Aer Lingus plane arriving.

In my mind I pictured the Owens family as they were when Karl and I had visited Ireland in 1972. I envisioned Darragh's younger sister, a small girl probably with red pigtails about ten or eleven. What I was supposed to do with this child, I had no idea. But I had been asked to help, and help I would.

Karl and I bought a balloon and a giant lollipop and went out to the airport to greet her. We waited and waited as person after person piled out of the plane. But there was no sign of a small, pig-tailed girl.

Instead, off the airplane, walking straight toward us, was a vision out of MTV. There must be a kind way to describe Catherine, but I can't think of it offhand. All I can say is she was no ten-year-old. She was all of about twenty-five, and somehow we had just inherited her!

Catherine had jet black hair spiked in the most bizarre arrangement I had ever seen. Her skirt, a micromini over long black-and-white striped stockings, was Day Glo green. Her shirt was iridescent orange. Her feet sported flat black boots, and perched on the back of her head was a black beret.

"Don't worry," she said, sensing our chagrin. "I'm here to seek my fame and fortune as an artist."

So in moved Catherine. It turned out that she had won a grant from an arts council in Ireland to work as an artist in America.

Initially I visualized delicate little watercolors, painted by a proper Irish colleen. But as it turned out, Catherine had to be *begged* to do anything small.

Once we arrived home from St. Louis to find one of her giant canvases stretched across the living-room wall. Broad swatches of color were splashed across the surface, and the smell of paint permeated the room. As creative as this massive *oeuvre* was, it had to go.

"Catherine," I said firmly, "you can't do this here. You have to do it in the back bedroom." From then on Catherine's paintings were the size of the bedroom wall. Here was a real case of art imitating life. It was art according to the size of the room in which the artist worked!

Catherine stayed three years, until we convinced her that she needed the influence of the art world in SoHo. Once she moved out, her sister, Sarah, moved in.

"This is where it's happening," she said as she stepped off the plane from Dublin. She wasn't able to tell me exactly *what* was happening, but she was sure it was here.

That was in 1987—and she still calls our home her own!

To the outside world it seems that the Soderlund family is very large and that we must have some wonderful Irish roots. But there isn't a hint of Irish in either Karl's or my background. The only thing we can claim is a lot of blarney!

How did I inherit these children of my ex-husband's friends? I can't explain what it is that draws young people like Catherine and Sarah into our lives on a regular basis.

All I know is that off the air or on, I can't resist animals or young people. That's why I was willing to stick my neck out one night on radio to get help for a teenager in trouble.

I was doing my radio show from my hotel in St. Louis one night when I got a call from a fourteen-year-old girl who had run away from home.

Her father had abused her, she said, and her mother, a prostitute, didn't want anything to do with her.

She had seen me on television and was calling from a phone booth in the middle of a deserted park.

"You're the only one I know who can help me," she said in a frightened voice.

I knew I had only one choice. I had to help the girl even if it meant breaking a cardinal journalistic rule: "Don't get involved."

I was already involved. She had called me for help, and I was her only hope. That's what I thought, anyway. So, I asked the producer what city she was calling from. As usual, the producer had gotten this information from the girl before her call was put through to me.

Now you have to realize that hundreds of phone calls come into the station every night from all over the country. The girl could have been in any city in the United States. But by an incredible coincidence, she was calling from a phone booth right there in the middle of a park in St. Louis! And I knew exactly where the park was.

"Go find her, Karl," I said.

Karl got to the phone booth, but the girl was too scared to come out. She had no idea who this man was, gesturing to her and telling her that "Sally sent me."

Through the police Karl arranged for a social worker to

come get her, and for the moment, at least, the girl was in good hands. Not long after, her father was arrested.

Even after the phone call was over, and I knew the girl was safe, I felt compelled to follow up on her case. Behind the scenes we made sure that she was placed in a good foster home.

Several months later she gave us a call. She loved her foster family, she said, and was even taking piano lessons. As for her parents, her father had committed suicide, but in all those months her mother had never once tried to contact her. Still, she was content with her new life and was undergoing therapy to help her face the future.

If she ever had problems again, she said, she knew exactly whom to call.

I always felt good about that girl and the way her situation turned out. In a way she gave a sense of meaning to all the commuting I was doing. Karl and I had been able to give some stability to this girl's life because we happened to be in St. Louis at the right time.

That was the silver lining to the cloud that commuting cast over our lives. Somehow just knowing that we were helping someone made the separation from my own kids a little more bearable.

Fortunately for my family there were more silver linings ahead.

Commuting may have undercut the stability of my own family life, but in a funny way, it also brought us closer together. Instead of hating every plane trip and every mile that separated us, we tried to turn the negative into a positive and started counting the miles toward free frequent flier bonuses on the airlines.

Soon it became a contest. "How many more miles do we have to fly before we have a ticket to Timbuktu?" I'd ask Karl. Even the kids got into the spirit.

"Here's the deal," we said to the kids. "You each get to choose where you want to go on vacation." I knew this was a surefire way to appeal to their well-honed senses of adventure.

From the time the children were small, Karl and I had made a priority out of travel with the family. Back in our Puerto Rico days we'd wake up one morning and announce, "We're going on a trip!" Then, without telling the children our destination, we'd pack up our bags, head for the airport, and fly to some island or other for a few days in the sun.

Over the years the kids grew so accustomed to spontaneous travel arrangements that they were always ready for anything. They warmed immediately to the idea of choosing their own adventures.

J.J. picked Japan. So in the winter of 1985 we flew to Tokyo for an Oriental experience that none of us will ever forget.

We got our first taste of Japanese hospitality in the *ofuro* baths in Hakone, a mountain resort outside Tokyo. The baths were typically Japanese, a communal arrangement with separate baths for men and women. Karl and J.J. headed for the male baths, and while Allison stayed back in her room, Andrea and I went to the female baths.

The baths consisted of a large room with a huge tub the size of a small swimming pool. In the room, squatting and scrubbing themselves in front of individual faucets, were fifty naked Japanese women, ranging in age from two months to a hundred years.

Neither Andrea nor I had on a stitch of clothes, and as we stepped nude into this Japanese inner sanctum, we absolutely stopped traffic. Every eye in the place was on us.

"Don't move," I said to Andrea. "Let them look at us."

"If you think I'm going to just stand here, you're crazy," she screamed back at me. "I don't like to be stared at."

"Andrea, please, just stand there, and in a few minutes they'll see that we're just the same as they are and stop staring. Then we'll wash ourselves, get in the tub, and do whatever they do."

Andrea relented, and a few minutes later the women stopped staring and we started scrubbing.

We may have managed to go native in the baths, but trying to do like the Japanese do on New Year's Eve was another story. We were in Kyoto, the cultural capital of Japan, on this most auspicious day of the Japanese calendar. You have to understand that to the Japanese, New Year's Eve takes on spiritual significance. It's not just a time to whoop and holler and celebrate, but a time to look forward to a year of good luck. The way you ensure that fortune will smile upon you is to go to a Shinto temple and pay homage to the spirits.

So we went, along with about two million other people, to one of Kyoto's main Shinto shrines. When we first arrived, everyone seemed very orderly, just the opposite of the raucous crowds in Times Square. It was just like the Japanese, I thought, for two million people to be standing quietly on line ten abreast in front of this temple.

We walked forward slowly, along with the crowd, for about two hours, when suddenly the atmosphere changed radically. For no apparent reason the crowd began to move even faster. I knew we were getting closer to the shrine because I could see the signs over the temple and some arches and things.

Without any warning the crowd started to surge forward. They were stampeding, like a bunch of wild English soccer fans. The din was unbelievable.

"Hold on to each other!" I yelled to Karl and the kids.

All around us, in this virtual sea of humanity, people were pushing and shoving. The next thing I knew, I looked down and saw blood all over the ground. Someone was being trampled!

Frantically I looked around for Karl and the kids. In the commotion, we had lost hold of each other, and now they were nowhere to be found. There was no Karl, no J.J., no

Allison, and no Andrea. I vaguely saw someone who looked like Karl about twenty feet away, but if it was Karl, he didn't see me.

All of a sudden I felt a tremendous shove, and I fell to the ground—on *top* of the woman whose blood I had seen a little while before. Screams were everywhere, but mine was the loudest.

"Help!" I screamed. "I'm being trampled!"

I heard a whistle, and into the crowd surged about a hundred riot police. They were all little guys with Darth Vader helmets and clubs, and they were whacking and screaming at everyone in their path.

Two of them came straight toward me and grabbed me up out of the crush. The next thing I knew, I was lying on the ground with hundreds of other people, who were being guarded by riot police. A Red Cross worker was darting among us, trying to patch people up.

"Sally! Sally!" I heard Karl scream.

"I'm over here," I yelled back.

When he and the kids found me, I was roughed up and scratched but not seriously hurt. But I was scared out of my wits.

What saved me, I think, was screaming in English at the top of my lungs. Maybe that's what alerted the riot police to my plight. Whatever it was, I was thankful to be alive. The next day the newspapers reported that five people had died in the riots at the temple. I still have a panicky feeling in any crowd.

One thing I know about my travel plans in the future: I don't think we're going to be visiting too many Japanese temples on New Year's Eve—no matter how interesting a cultural experience it may be.

I'll stick to massages in Macao. After I had been nearly killed in Kyoto, a little rest and rehabilitation in the Portuguese colony seemed like a good idea. When I announced to Karl that I was going for a massage in our hotel, he said, "We'll come with you."

The sign in the lobby said HEALTH CLUB, but when we opened the door, my health suddenly gave out. There, behind a glass window, were thirteen young girls sitting in a row. They all had on black leotards and little white skirts, and each was holding a number. They looked ready for a lot more than a back rub.

J.J. said, "Mom, who are those girls?"

Andrea said, "Shut up, J.J."

Karl said, "Look at thaaat!"

I said, "I'm not getting a massage. Forget the whole thing."

China seemed tame by comparison. Actually we hadn't planned to go to China. The trip just happened, the way things often do when we're on the road together. We had stopped over in Hong Kong, and after we had seen everything from the junks in Aberdeen to the views from Victoria Peak, we put our knapsacks on our backs and headed for the Chinese border.

With no guide, no tour, no anything, we marched into China as though it were Chinatown. Nobody bothered us or stopped us. Maybe that's because we each had a "Hello! My name is Sally" name tag on our shirts just to look friendly.

There were no taxis or cars for hire, so we hopped into a dilapidated public bus and decided to go wherever it took us.

We ended up in a little town in South China with a restaurant where absolutely nobody spoke English. That, of course, only added to the fun. Next, we jumped on a bus that dropped us off in a little village that had no electricity. One of the villagers invited us into his home and asked the neighbors around for a "look-see."

Now some people wouldn't enjoy being gawked at in the middle of a foreign country. But not us. We crave that kind of camaraderie; in fact, we seek it out. To make friends wherever we go, we always take presents—balloons, ball-point pens—and a Polaroid camera for instant photos. We handed out these gifts like crazy to all our newfound Chinese friends. Once they saw the results of the Polaroids, they were only too happy to pose for more pictures.

As I look through the photo albums from that trip, there's a picture of us surrounded by curious Chinese. Right next to it is another photo, though, that's a reminder to me that even on the other side of the earth, my mind was never far from broadcasting.

In the photo, I'm in a Chinese temple, lighting thirty joss sticks. They're supposed to bring good fortune, which is what I've been betting on all my life.

I've always been one of the world's greatest candle lighters. I'll walk into a church and see the votive candles, and if one candle will do, I figure a hundred will do better. The way I see it, if I'm going to bet on success, why not set the world on fire while I'm doing it?

That's why in every cathedral I've ever visited, from Notre Dame to St. Patrick's, I have given my money, and one by one, I've started lighting candles. In fact, I've almost torched some of the world's greatest cathedrals that way.

Just to be certain I'm on the side of the angels, I always cover all religious bases. In that Buddhist temple in China I burned joss sticks until the place smelled like an incense factory.

All those joss sticks must have worked because from the time we got back from our Oriental odyssey, my television show was on a roll. By 1987 we had become so successful that we were able to move the production of *Sally Jessy Raphaël* to New Haven, which is only a stone's throw from New York City.

I guess you could say that good fortune was indeed smiling. My commute was commuted—to a limousine ride!

CHAPTER THIRTEEN

Behind the Scenes in TV Talk

TELEVISION IS ALWAYS A GAMBLE. No matter how successful a show is, from minute to minute it's a gamble of creativity, a gamble of ratings, and a gamble of instinct.

After years in this business I've finally learned that there's not a lot of rhyme or reason to why one show is a blockbuster and another a bust. You're either a success or you're not, and if you are doing well, you might as well go for broke!

Some incredibly bizarre things happen on *Sally Jessy Raphaël*, not necessarily because we've planned it but because we take the risk of allowing it to happen.

But what you see on your television screen is only part of the picture. Often it's what's going on *off camera* that's the most bizarre of all.

We did a show on nudists not long ago. You've got it. Honest-to-goodness red-blooded naked nudists. Of course, I was prepared for what was coming. In fact, it was my idea. I had told our executive producer, Burt Dubrow, "Let's get a group of people who feel comfortable about their bodies to tell us what it really feels like." Nudists fit into that category.

I knew that some people would think that the idea was beyond the bounds of good taste. But I also knew that the idea was inherently fascinating. Most of us are so uncomfortable with the bodies we've been born with that we are endlessly complaining or covering or adapting or exercising. On the other hand, there are really people in this world who are so comfortable in their skins that they could sit naked in front of a TV camera and a live audience without an ounce of self-consciousness.

The closest I ever came to it, personally, was the day Karl and I showed up for a friend's dinner party without a stitch of clothing under our trench coats. The looks on their faces when they came to take our coats were almost worth the fact that they never spoke to us again. Before the dinner they had said, "Don't dress," and we had simply taken them literally.

So I was prepared to face the nudists. We had planned the program down to the last detail. The cameraman was going to shoot from the neck up, so the audience at home would see only their faces.

The day of the show the studio audience took its place, and Burt warmed them up with folksy humor, as he always does. Then the five nudists walked onto the set— stark naked—to take their places facing the audience.

Finally it was my turn to walk out. I breezed through the door, took my place among the audience facing the guests, and realized I had met my match.

There, staring me in the face at eye level, were five crotches. The one thing we hadn't planned for in all our preparations was the height of the stage. If they had been at ground level, I would have simply been looking each guest in the eye. Instead, I had a gynecologist's view of life.

Meanwhile, the show started, and inside I was secretly doubled over with laughter. But I knew I had to get out of the situation or I wouldn't be able to carry on. I had to get to a place onstage where I could look at their faces. I couldn't just keep staring at their private parts—their *really* private parts. Otherwise it was going to blow my mind.

Eventually I got up onstage with them, and we talked face-to-face. The wonderful thing about the show was that except for one man, they had really potty bodies. If you looked beyond the ratings factor—the sensationalism of the program—you saw what I hoped people would see: a group of people whose bodies were far from perfect and who couldn't care less about what other people thought.

Afterward, of course, it seemed as if everybody in America wanted to know how I felt about interviewing nudists. The truth is, I didn't feel anything. I'm not someone who has a problem with nudity. I'm married to a man whose ethnic background is Scandinavian and who has absolutely no problem with nudity. He's never covered up, even in front of our own daughters. We have what would be for America an extreme Scandinavian attitude toward nudity. So I don't think or feel anything about it, one way or another.

Needless to say, the ratings were high that day. So was the press coverage. Every wire service picked up the story. Ironically, after all the shows I've done with intrinsic value to try to change the world, the one that generated the most publicity was the nudist show.

If publicity comes your way, and you need it, and you're not that famous, and you don't have a big budget, you ride it and take it. So I took the publicity. The news story wasn't what the camera had revealed but what it had kept hidden.

Just as the camera covered up the bare facts about those nudists, sometimes it also hides my insecurities.

On television I'm always ready for any kind of derring-do. In fact, my favorite shows are those Walter Mitty-like adventures that stretch me to do things I wouldn't get to do on my own. I'll get down and dirty with female wrestlers, put on boxing gloves and go for a round, or do a turn around the rink with Roller Derby queens. Somehow, over the years, I've managed to pull off dozens of physically demanding stunts. As a result, on camera I can look almost invincible.

But inside I don't feel quite so courageous. Even though I'm a major risk taker, I, like anyone else, have second thoughts. The difference between me and most other people, though, is that my second thoughts come *after* I've embarked on some foolhardy exploit, rather than before!

On one show I roller-skated with the Bay City Bombers, a group of Roller Derby queens. I practiced for two days straight before I felt ready to hit the rink. Once the show got rolling, there were a few shaky moments when I had second thoughts: "What if I fall? What if the skaters behind me roll over me?"

But it was already too late. The camera was zooming in on me, and I had no choice but to zoom around with the best of them.

Then there was the time I got in the ring with the Girls of Glow, a group of female wrestlers. Before the show we worked out a routine so I knew exactly what was going to happen to me. One of the wrestlers would twirl me around and then throw me to the mat. They rehearsed the whole act and taught me how to fall so I wouldn't kill myself.

It all seemed simple enough, until we got on the air. One of the wrestlers held me up over her head, and as she spun me around, my mind started spinning with the possibilities of a mishap. "If I don't hit the mat in exactly the right way in a second and a half, I'll be flattened Sally."

Then I remembered the camera. It was on me, and I had to play my part. At that moment I wasn't just Sally. I was one of the Girls of Glow. I landed like a pro and accepted the kudos of the crowd.

What saves my neck in these situations is the presence of the camera. There's an almost human quality about the camera that gives me a sense of security. When I know the camera is on me, I put on the show of my life with the confidence that I'll be safe from harm.

But when the camera is hidden, and I can't feel its warm eye upon me, my insecurities are laid bare. That's when I can become vulnerable to my own vivid imagination and fears.

The night I walked the streets of New York with a prostitute was one of those times. It wasn't my idea to go out on Forty-second Street on a cold night in the middle of March dressed like a hooker. But the producers wanted me to do it.

I went along with the idea because every single time I've done a show on prostitutes, one of the women has made this comment: "You can never know how we feel. You've got a nice apartment and a nice family. You have no idea what our lives are like."

By golly, they were never going to be able to say that again! Of course, I couldn't share the experience of going to a hotel with a man. Picking up a "john" would be illegal—and besides, that wasn't my line of work. But I could stand on a gritty street corner in the middle of Times Square and start to feel the fear.

So I hit the street with a prostitute the producers had lined up. She was an articulate thirtyish woman, with frizzy red hair. Why she was willing to subject herself to the scrutiny of the camera, I'm not really sure.

Perhaps she was an activist type, one of those who are in what I like to call the Hookers' Benevolent League, fighting to legalize the world's oldest profession. Or perhaps she fell into the "It's gonna make me a star" category. They're the kind that says, "This is all show biz! I'm not really a hooker! I hook to make money; but I'm really a grade B actress, and I want to get on television and be famous."

Whatever her reasons for being on the show, she was more than happy to help me out. While the camera rolled, she dressed me up in a tight miniskirt, heavy makeup, and a sequined jacket, and off we went into the night.

The minute I got on the street, though, I realized it was the most dumb-foolish thing I'd ever done in my career.

First of all, it was cold. My friend the hooker had on a fur coat, but I was standing out on the street in a flimsy jacket and miniskirt.

Second, I was beginning to get scared. My protective shield—the TV camera—was concealed in a nearby van recording all my moves. As far as I was concerned, it was *too* concealed. Without the camera in front of me, I felt exposed and vulnerable.

My mind went into high gear. Before long I was picturing myself in the midst of a sleazy movie with one lurid scenario after another. In one scene an irate pimp thought I was horning in on his territory. In another, a prostitute became outraged because some upstart celebrity —me—seemed to be making a mockery of her profession. Then my mind leaped to a logical conclusion as I pictured one of them walking right up to me and sticking a shiv in my rib cage before the cameraman knew what had happened.

Fortunately some fans brought me back to reality. Every now and then someone would drive by in his car and yell out, "Hiya, Sally!" Then I would breathe a sigh of relief and continue my chilly vigil.

During my four hours on the street a few men *did* walk by and proposition me. But I never gave them even a verbal tumble—since I might have ended up in the clinker with a lot of explaining to do. In the end the only film footage we could use, for legal reasons, was a simulated encounter using an actor.

As far as I'm concerned, I'd just as soon forget the whole episode. What I'll never erase from my memory, though, is the potential for danger for those without the protection of the camera. If that's what it's like for the "women of the night," they all deserve our prayers.

Shows about prostitutes and nudists are, of course, guaranteed to be titillating and will inevitably draw in more viewers than a panel of "talking heads"—experts on some subject or other. That's predictable.

What isn't predictable, though, is the response of the public on any given day to any television program—even one that's provocative. There are so many variables at work in the ratings game that nothing is a certainty in this business.

On most days the ratings are more like roulette. I could do the greatest television program in the world, but if the show that goes on before mine in a particular city is deadly dull, people will switch to another channel or switch off before *Sally Jessy Raphaël* comes on. As a result, I will not inherit any viewers, and in fact, I'll lose viewers I might have had.

This is what's called "flow" in television lingo—a term that refers to the strength of your lineup, the quality of the shows coming before and after yours. The flow is in the hands of a local TV station, *not* in the hands of a Burt Dubrow producing *Sally Jessy Raphaël*. Burt's job is to create a product. The local station determines when it's televised.

The flow of shows can also work to your advantage. For argument's sake, let's say you're on before *The Cosby Show* in some cities. Everybody wants to see *Cosby*, so during the last half of your show people will be tuning in like crazy to get ready for the sitcom. It doesn't matter what your program is about. The viewers' sets are on, and you get good ratings because of the show that comes after yours.

Weather can play a role in the ratings, too. On a beautiful spring day in the East, my ratings might drop because everybody decided to go out and ride a bike. During a blizzard in the Midwest my ratings might soar because everyone is sitting around the TV set, keeping cozy and warm.

Then there are the times my show is preempted and my ratings aren't really mine at all. One day I might look at my ratings in Boston and see that a particular show that I thought would do well did even better: The ratings go through the roof! But before I pat myself on the back for a job well done, I have to look at what actually happened in Boston that day. In fact, it's possible my show wasn't on at all; it may have been preempted by a major news story of a race riot in Roxbury that pulls in every viewer in the city. So I would get the ratings of the race riot!

If you think this is absurd, consider what happened to my radio ratings in New York City one season. My talk show was carried by the same station that broadcast the Yankee games. Whenever the game ran too long, my show was preempted as long as the game went on. On those days I got the ratings of the New York Yankees.

What's even more frustrating is to work hard on a show and know that in some cities it will never be a hit because I'm opposite the hottest game show of the moment. I can fly into the city, talk to the press, promote my show like crazy on commercials, and nothing will boost the ratings. Absolutely nothing. There is no way I can hope to beat the number one game show.

When I'm on the air opposite some other game show, at least I have a fighting chance—except when a contestant is on a winning streak or the show is giving away especially fabulous prizes. Then my ratings go down. If the contestants are boring or if the prizes are run-of-the-mill, my ratings go up.

So now you know what we're up against.

There are those in this business who will tell you that they know exactly what it takes to create a hit television show. Don't believe a word they say. If anyone knew the secrets to success in television, he'd be king. The truth is, what you see on television—on my show as well as on Bill Cosby's—is nothing more than an educated guess about what will go over with the viewers.

From what I've seen, Burt Dubrow is the closest you can get to a seer in television. His eye and ear are the best in the business. He's a child of the TV screen, and he understands the medium better than anyone else I know. But even Burt would never claim to have all the answers to what works in television.

Since there's no way to predict accurately what America wants to watch every day, we have to be flexible and broad-minded in the kinds of programs we present. I can't presume to be an arbiter of taste, and frankly I don't even try. If we did shows only about what I'm interested in, we'd have a steady diet of programs on wine tasting, model train collecting, and quilting. With that kind of programming I know exactly where I'd end up: shooting the show in my backyard with only Karl as my audience!

So that's why Burt, the producers, and I keep trying to cover our bases. We go for the stories of heartbreak, of courage, and of triumph over adversity, and occasionally we throw in a zinger—like the program on prostitutes—to make everybody stand up and take notice.

No matter how offensive a topic may be to some people, though, I've learned to appear nonjudgmental. Thanks to Burt Dubrow's direction, I'm getting good at masking my feelings. If a man confesses to me that he's having an affair, I don't jump down his throat or say that he's a dirty rotten scoundrel—even if that's what's on my mind. Instead, I listen and sympathize and try to put myself in his shoes. With that approach you almost always get more out of a guest. Inevitably he feels so accepted and comfortable he's willing to tell me just about anything.

Behind my mask of tolerance, though, a war of emotions sometimes rages. Like my audience at home, I'm often genuinely torn over what my position should be on a given subject. The day a group of topless dancers appeared on the show, a part of me wanted desperately to tell them off. But I couldn't and didn't because I couldn't quite figure out what I believed.

Unlike the nudists who let it all hang out, the young go-go dancers on the set that day didn't show up topless. In fact, some were dressed downright demurely. To a viewer at home, any one of them could have been the girl next door—until she stood up and danced.

One of the young women came out wearing nothing but a black bikini and felt fedora and "demonstrated" her dance style. Believe me, it wasn't rock and roll.

Night after night these lovely ladies earned their living dancing topless in front of all-male audiences. They willingly gyrated, postured, and flaunted their bare breasts at those bug-eyed guys and then took the money and ran.

What's more, not one of them had one bit of remorse over her job choice. They all found the job a "turn-on." That's what threw me.

They weren't poor souls telling me, "I'm forced to dance to feed my family," or, "I'm doing this, but it's terrible." Instead, they were boasting about their talents. Each and every one of them said, "I love walking in the limelight, I have a wonderful body, and it's fun showing off!"

With those kinds of attitudes, it was hard for me to work up sympathy for them. How could I feel sorry for someone who didn't think there was anything to be sorry about? How could I feel compassionate toward a woman whose occupation I found repugnant? Yet who was I to judge?

My mind was a jumble of contradictions. The feminist in me wanted to shake them and say, "Don't you realize you're setting the women's movement back two hundred years? You don't *have* to do this. You can find another way to make money."

The practical side of me argued: "What other way could they make two thousand dollars a week to pay the bills?" Some of the women were putting themselves

hrough college by dancing topless, and it certainly was a
quicker way to earn a buck than working at a fast-food
ranchise. Others were working at night so they could be
home during the day with their children. How could I
quibble with those motives?

Then there was the side of me that said, "You can't
judge them because in a way you're selling out, too." Like
everyone else in television, I've had to make compromises
along the way to be a success. To stay alive in this business, I've had to do what's commercially viable, particu-
arly at ratings time. And I've had to adjust the way I look
and act in order to be the right image for television. Who
was I to tell these women not to dance with their clothes
off?

All this was going through my head during the show as
stood in the audience with a mike in my hand, but I
didn't let on what I was thinking.

In the end I kept quiet and let the audience speak for
me. I played off a feminist question from the audience
against a practical response from the dancers onstage, and
we ended up with a very balanced show. Perhaps the show
was too balanced, and I really should have stepped in. In
some cases, to be completely frank with you, I'm still not
sure where I stand.

There was one program, though, where I knew without
a doubt that I *had* to interject my opinion, even if it went
against the plan.

The show was Burt Dubrow's idea. He had been home
watching the news one Sunday night when a segment
came on that piqued his interest. Two little children in
North Carolina had been suspended from school for
preaching.

Now this was not just a case of two little kids with sweet
smiles on their faces passing out Bibles to their classmates.
These kids were preaching hellfire and brimstone from
the top of their lungs. From the mouths of these babes,

children and teachers alike were being damned to perdi-
tion.

Burt took one look at the news reports and knew we
had to have these kids and their parents on the show.
Monday morning he charged into the office and said to
the staff, "I don't care what it takes. Get the family. Get
the mother, get the father, and get the kids!"

Two days later they were in our New Haven studio.

Here's how we did it. First, Burt assigned one of our
four staff producers to the story. It's the producer's job to
orchestrate a show from start to finish. The producer in
charge of the preacher show tracked down the family and
"booked" them for a particular taping session in New
Haven. Once the travel and hotel arrangements were all
set, she then proceeded to research the story in depth.
Next, she spent a couple of hours on the telephone
"preinterviewing" the mother and father, to determine
the approach I should take in my questioning.

On the basis of the preinterview the producer then
drew up a list of suggested questions, along with an intro-
duction I could use for the story.

On the day of the show we added another step because
of the inflammatory nature of the broadcast. Usually the
guests wait in what we call the green room, relaxing before the show, while I stay in my dressing room until show
time. This time Burt invited the family into his office for a
"chat." He wanted to find out for himself what made the
father tick. He never did figure it out.

Right before taping time Burt came into my dressing
room, shaking his head. "This guy's gonna be tough," he
warned me. He advised me to home in on the issue of
education because the man was adamantly opposed to
sending his kids to college for fear that their minds would
become warped.

Finally, show time arrived, and it was all up to me. I
walked out on the set ready for anything—and I got it!

Once on the air, those same children who had been

shouting tirades in front of their school barely said a word. Although I tried to be very gentle with them and concentrated on ordinary questions about their lives, they had no responses. But the minute I asked them to "preach," each one stood up and, as if by rote, launched into a well-practiced Elmer Gantry routine.

It was chilling to witness firsthand. These weren't kids who had some inner drive to spread the Word of God. They were more like robots, who could be automated on command. It was clear to me that these poor kids had been terribly manipulated by their parents.

As for their father, he could converse only in biblical quotations—most of them accusatory. Now, it's certainly admirable to have a knowledge of the Bible. But he was using the Bible as a weapon—to admonish all who listened to him. He didn't display any love, he apparently didn't know people, and he certainly wouldn't answer a direct question. Like his children, he gave only rote responses that projected a total lack of respect for whoever was listening.

His attitude was inflammatory enough on run-of-the-mill topics. But when he started attacking the pope for being a child molester, I knew I had to do something. Our studio audience in New Haven that day was predominantly Catholic, and I could see that they were up in arms. The way things were going, the whole show could end up in a street fight if I didn't step in.

So, I walked right up to him, and face-to-face I let him have it. "Number one, I'm worried about what you're doing to your children," I said. "Number two, I cannot tolerate a belief in God who is not a God of love or is not a God who loves children. I find your attitude abominable."

I knew in my bones that the situation had become so uncomfortable that the audience was begging me to take a stand. Usually my opinions can be too strong for the living rooms of America. But in this case my instincts told me I had to speak up, or I would be letting my viewers down. They didn't want to see a free-for-all on the set. Still, they did want me to tell this man what was right and what was wrong. And what was wrong was how he was treating his children.

In response to my criticisms, the man said I was damned as in Genesis 13. My future, it seemed, was like that of Sodom and Gomorrah!

But I'm more than willing to take the heat if my instincts are right, and in this case I know they were. No matter how much I may have offended this man, I couldn't stand mute and let him destroy others right before my eyes.

He couldn't have been too offended, though, because not long afterward he agreed to appear on my show again —this time on location in his hometown, surrounded by an audience of his irate neighbors. There was enough electricity in the air that day to keep the whole city in lights for a decade.

With most of my guests, however, my job is not to preach but to be a catalyst for catharsis. My ultimate aim is to draw them out and stimulate them to say the things they want to disclose—even if it's painful.

One young woman appeared on the show with her ex-husband, who had deserted her for a gay life-style. With this couple I didn't talk about right or wrong. I talked about feelings: how she felt when he left her with two small children to care for; how he felt as he sat next to her that day, hearing about the hardships of her life and learning from her own lips how much he had hurt her.

The more they talked, the more I sensed their profound sadness over their shattered lives. So I asked about love: whether she still loved him and whether, if ever, he had loved her.

In one poignant moment of truth the man tried to give her something to hold on to—as if it could change the circumstances of their lives.

"You are the only woman I ever loved," he said to her ently. "And I still love you."

Tears came to the young woman's eyes, and she bravely ied to hold back the emotions surging within her. Inside was crying, too.

You may be wondering, as I always have, why a woman ke this would agree to come on national television and xpose herself to more hurt and rejection from the man he so desperately loved. And why would this man, who ooked dapper and fit, put his new life on the line to ppear on my show with his obviously downtrodden ex-ife?

After years of interviewing, I've come to the conclusion hat the reason many guests are willing to come on my how is that they have a deep, overpowering need to share ome awful experience that happened to them. In the haring, they apparently hope to reach some ultimate res-lution of their dilemma. They want to take these lemons n their lives and make lemonade.

I've found that wives who have been beaten, children ho have been abused, and victims who have been left for ead want to believe that the terrible things that were erpetrated on them were not just senseless acts. Instead, hey want to confirm that there is a lesson to be learned y their suffering—a lesson that transforms their negative xperience into a positive force for good.

I sense that this is true because a majority of guests on ally Jessy Raphaël do not get paid for appearing. The only nes who are paid are a tiny fraction who might be mem-ers of some union that demands that they get compen-ated. What's more, most are not plugging a book.

For some guests, appearing on the show does represent conscious risk. A few of our guests even appear in dis-uise, with wigs and makeup concealing their true identi-ies. We've even gone so far as to change their names for heir own protection.

Certainly there are people, like the father of the

preacher kids, who think that being on television will somehow promote their cause. But the vast majority of guests are ordinary people who simply want to tell their stories—not for self-aggrandizement, or so that they can get famous, but because it might save someone else from disaster.

They just want to say to others, "This is what happened to me. Learn from it. Hear the lessons, and be careful." Most of all, they want to be a source of encouragement and explain how they got out of their crisis.

So that's why people appear on television. From what I've seen, most Americans do *not* want to be famous for fifteen minutes, as Andy Warhol may have thought.

Unless you're Sylvester Stallone's mother.

Luckily for me, Jacqueline Stallone absolutely adores the limelight. Whenever she appears on my show, I know I can count on some fireworks.

Not long ago, for example, we did a show on celebrity mothers that looked like it would be a winner. We had booked some of the biggest names in motherhood. The mothers of Cher, Sly Stallone, Patrick Swayze, Sammy Davis, Jr., and Cybill Shepherd all were on hand in New Haven to talk about their famous kids. The show was tailor-made for gossip and fun, and I felt there was no way I could miss.

But fifteen minutes into the show I could tell from the look on Burt's face that something was terribly wrong. During a commercial break he pulled me aside and whispered, "Your energy level's too low. The show is dragging. You've got to step it up."

I knew I had to do something fast to keep the show alive.

One thing that's important to understand about TV shows like mine and Phil's and Oprah's and Geraldo's is that what you see is pretty much what you get. In my case we sometimes tape two different shows, an hour each, back to back in one day. Because of the cost of producion, we can't afford to tape much longer than the hour per show we're allotted. That means that very little is edited out.

On shows like 20/20, 60 Minutes, or one of Barbara Walters's specials, on the other hand, the star reporters and their staffs can spend hours interviewing guests. Most of those hours never make it to the television screen. If the star is having a bad day, or if the guest gives a boring response, that segment is dropped. As a result, what the viewer gets is a fabulous interview that appears to be spontaneous, with provocative questions and lively answers.

But we don't have the luxury of time or editing to make the show better. It has to happen at the moment, or it doesn't happen. So when Burt told me I was slow on the uptake with the celebrity mothers, I knew I had to change the pace and start off the next segment of the show with a bang.

There was only one person who could do the job: Jacqueline Stallone. With her flashing eyes, jet black hair, ruby lips, and crimson nails, she was a hot ticket. Not only did she look sensational, but I knew from experience that she was a sure bet to say something outrageous as well.

So, as soon as we went back on the air after the commercial break, I threw her a question about her love life.

Her rejoinder was a showstopper: "Let me introduce you to my boyfriend; he's in the studio audience." With that a distinguished gray-haired gentleman stood up and waved obligingly to the camera.

The only problem was that he was married—and to someone else!

The show never slowed down after that.

CHAPTER FOURTEEN

A Day in the Life

A DAY IN MY LIFE is like the Indianapolis 500. You keep going around the turns and never stop moving until the flag goes down at the finish line, signaling that the race is over. There's rarely a moment for a pit stop. If something's not quite right, I don't have time to think. I just have to keep my engines revved up and my mind focused on getting through.

With me, there's no such thing as a typical day. The only relative constants during the past few years have been my TV tapings in New Haven on Mondays, Tuesdays, and Wednesdays and my nightly radio broadcasts. Since we moved production of my TV show to New York in 1989, I've added an extra day of TV tapings to my routine. But even these scheduled events aren't always fixed. So, I have to wake up each day ready for unexpected demands—and surprises.

6:45 A.M.: I get up at my country house in northern Westchester. I bought the house a few years ago as an escape hatch from the pressures of the city. I call it Hare Hollow, and every place you look there's a fake rabbit staring out at you. Actually, though, the place is our hobbit hole, where we can settle back and feel totally at home. Our home is a woodsy enclave, where the only noises are the sounds of the birds and of Karl calling to me that it's time to get moving.

The first thing that passes my lips in the morning is grapefruit juice. I'm a big believer that grapefruit juice keeps you thin. Then I take a bunch of vitamins, and Karl and I get in our sweat clothes and drive to the local deli. We have a cup of coffee, spend a few minutes chatting with the neighbors, and drive half a block to the gym.

That's when my day really begins. I hit the Nautilus machines for a while, and then I go on to the treadmill for my major workout of the day. Sometimes I run on the treadmill, but mostly I walk so that I can listen to tapes at the same time.

While I'm exercising the body, I'm exercising my mind. I'm so time-conscious that every spare minute is spent doing something along with something else. But these are no ordinary tapes I listen to. Some are motivational tapes, subliminal motivational tapes. With these tapes, you hear only music, but underneath you are being primed with a powerful message to reprogram your mind.

I'm not trying to reprogram myself to quit smoking or anything practical like that, even though I'm convinced it works. Karl, who was a confirmed "dessertaholic," completely lost his interest in desserts after a month of listening to a subliminal tape on the subject.

What I'm trying to do is start my day with positive, "can-do" attitudes. In broadcasting, it's so easy to be deflated each day. I can open a paper and see a story on another talk show host and start feeling unloved and dejected. Because this is such a subjective business, you need to know in your heart that you are good in order to withstand the negative external pressures you face day in and day out.

So I start my day with an upbeat tape such as *Thinking Big* or another called *Chop Wood, Carry Water*, done by Richard Thomas—John Boy of *The Waltons*.

With my mind filled with positive thoughts, I'm ready

to face the day. By the time I've finished my treadmill and tape routine, it's about 7:45 A.M., and we head back to the house to get ready for work.

8:00 A.M.: A company limousine picks Karl and me up at the door of the house and drives us to New York to tape my TV show. The ride to the studio takes an hour or more, and on the way I study the research and questions for the shows we're doing.

For the program on celebrity mothers, for example, I spent a good deal of time reading clips from the tabloids for tidbits of gossip to weave into the show. I also perused the producer's research notes, trying to get a feel for each woman's personality.

During the limousine ride I found out that Cher's mother had had a face-lift and that she didn't have a boyfriend at the moment. I learned that Patrick Swayze's mother was a pro who not only had taught him how to dance but had been in show business all her life. She had choreographed *Urban Cowboy* with John Travolta. That was a signal to me that she knew the ropes in this business and wouldn't be star-struck.

Cybill Shepherd's mom, on the other hand, was a sweet southern lady from Memphis who lived in a world apart from show business. When the producer called her for a preinterview, she had been in her backyard with Cybill and the twin babies, having a real family get-together. To her Cybill wasn't a "star." She was her daughter, who had just had these wonderful babies, and wasn't it fun that they were all visiting Grandma!

The way Cybill's mom looked at things, *I* was the celebrity. She listened to my radio show regularly, and she was pleased as punch to be going on my TV show and getting her hair done and wasn't this all going to be grand.

9:00 A.M.: The limousine pulls into the studio, and I spend fifteen minutes meeting with Burt Dubrow. Next come forty-five minutes for hair, done by Richard, who's great, then makeup, and briefings by the producers of the two shows that are scheduled that day. Just before show time Burt warms up the audience, and then, to enthusiastic applause, I breeze into the studio and take over. I'll banter with the crowd a few minutes, and then the show begins.

11:00 A.M.: We're on the air until noon, with short breaks for commercials. During those brief interludes Burt can fill me in on any problems that need correction. On Tuesdays we tape two shows, so when the first show is finished, I run back to my dressing room, change clothes, have my hair and makeup adjusted, and get a last-minute update by the producer of the next show. By 12:30 we're taping the second show with the same audience.

After the show, I stay at the studio for a while doing interviews or talking with Burt about the next day's schedule.

3:00 P.M.: I'm back in the limousine heading for Westchester. This time I spend the commute reading the newspaper, or speed-reading a book for the next day's program, or being interviewed—for this book, for example.

4:30 P.M.: This is my time to relax, take a nap, or just putter around the house. I never used to have time off until one day an argument over a coat hanger taught me a lesson about pacing myself.

I was getting dressed to go to an important meeting when Karl started pressuring me to get out the door. Instead of hustling to get out, I walked toward the closet to put away the hanger that had held my blouse.

"You don't have time to hang up the hanger," Karl yelled impatiently.

He was right. Our lives had been moving so fast that I had no time to hang up a clothes hanger! I knew that this couldn't be a good way to live if I couldn't even do a simple thing like that. So I vowed from then on to take some leisure time for myself every day.

These days we even have time to eat dinner. When we taped the TV show in New Haven, I'd get home with only forty-five minutes to spare before I had to go on the ABC radio network. I'd eat a quick salad to tide me over, and while I was eating, I'd think about what I was going to say to open the radio show. Now Karl has time to whip up some spaghetti and we can sit down and eat together before show time.

6:45 P.M.: Karl starts testing the radio equipment for the remote hookup in our living room. It's wired into the switchboard at the ABC studios in New York. I can hear the control room talking to me over my earphones, and I also have a speaker over which I can hear the caller's questions.

7:00 P.M.: For three hours, minus commercial breaks, I'm on the air, giving people advice. Sometimes we throw in an extra hour to cover a day when I might be on vacation or if an emergency arises. You have to be ready for anything, and we are.

One night I got home to discover that something was wrong with the radio hookup at my home. I couldn't hear a thing coming in from New York. So, while the minutes ticked away, the station had to send an engineer to Westchester to check on the problem. Meanwhile, my show had to be broadcast, so during the time it took to fix the connection, the station played one of the extra hours I had taped the week before. By 8:00 I was back on the air.

11:00 P.M.: The work day is finally over. Karl and I have a snack and unwind after a long day.

11:30 P.M.: It's time to touch base with the family. I put in a call to each of the kids, including Sarah in our apartment in New York. Some nights I also call Aunt Barrie in Seattle. She's my mother's younger sister, and since Dede died, she's become my surrogate mother. Aunt Barrie has taken up right where Dede left off: She follows my career, keeps a scrapbook of my exploits, and visits at least three times a year. A couple of years ago, we even went to Hawaii together.

By the time I've talked to Aunt Barrie, and J.J. has given me a rundown on his day at boarding school, and Allison has told me the story of her life, and Andrea has filled me in on her shiatsu massage lessons, and Sarah has told me how the dogs are doing and what's happening in the world of rock music, it's midnight.

Midnight: Karl and I collapse in the sauna for a while and then hit the hot tub, which is built into our outdoor patio. We've gone very California in the middle of Westchester. If any of our neighbors were up at that hour and peeked through the woods, they'd see a vision of two naked bodies streaking through the night.

I'm still so keyed up from the day's events that there's no way I can go to sleep. After the hot tub I'll watch a little bit of *Nightline,* which we tape, and maybe some of *Arsenio Hall* and only then do we go to sleep.

2:00 A.M.: The lights are out, and we are finally getting our beauty sleep—all four hours and forty-five minutes of it. Before I know it, it's 6:45 A.M. again, and we're ready for another day and another dollar.

Regular Daily Irregularities: Three nights a week I stay in Manhattan and do my radio show directly from the ABC studios. While I'm there, I tape commercials and special promotions for my show.

Thursdays and Fridays are always business days, doing what the rest of the world does: talking to my accountant or lawyer, having a doctor's appointment, shopping, having press interviews, or giving speeches.

One Friday I flew to Michigan to give a speech and got back in time to do my radio show at night.

Offbeat Business: I once figured out that I average one plane trip a week on show business appearances not directly related to my TV show. For example, every year without fail, I've done Sammy Davis, Jr.'s telethon in St. Louis for Variety Club International. That's a charity that was started more than ninety years ago by people in show business. When an orphan was left on the steps of a vaudeville house, the performers got together to pay for the child's education. That tradition has developed into a large organization with many child-oriented charities supported by musicians, vaudevillians, and even broadcasters. One of the most active chapters is the one in St. Louis.

I knew Sammy since my Puerto Rico days, and when I started doing my television show in St. Louis, he asked me to get involved. The first year I was on his telethon, I sang and danced. The second, I only sang. The third, I stopped singing, and for the last few years I've done nothing but beg for money.

Despite the fact that it's grueling and that you have to stay up all night and are exhausted the next day, it's worth the effort. Sammy knew almost everybody in show business, and through him I got to meet Liza Minnelli and Jerry Lewis. Jerry and I hit it off so well that he invited me to be on his Labor Day telethon.

None of these stars has to worry about me, though. I've finally figured out why I've become such a popular guest. At the end of the Variety Club telethon, as we all stood in front of the orchestra for the grand finale, one of Sammy's pals leaned over to me and said, "Can I stand behind you?"

"Yes," I said, flattered that he would want to be near

me during the closing song. "I must be pretty terrific," I thought as I flashed him a big smile.

Just as I was about to belt out the opening bars of the song, he confessed why he craved my companionship. "I really *have* to listen to you sing," he said. "You have the worst voice of any woman I have ever heard in my life. Next to you, I sound good!"

So that's why they want me on telethons!

Weekend Whimsy: Whenever I have a weekend free of show business obligations, I've discovered a foolproof way to keep myself from getting bored. In 1987 I bought a nineteenth-century country inn in Pennsylvania, which we run as a commercial bed-and-breakfast establishment.

If that sounds crazy, you have to understand that I have real estate-itis. This is a disease that afflicts people who believe that their surroundings are tremendously important. Maybe it comes from my theatrical background, but I think that our environment influences how we behave. If there's not enough morning light streaming through my windows, I become terribly depressed. If I look around my apartment and see nothing that pleases my eye, I get frustrated.

Karl is a different sort of person altogether. He could live in a cave and nothing about him would change.

But I have to keep changing my environment to be happy. So that's why, when I read in the paper that a highway was being completed in rural Bucks County, Pennsylvania, I told Karl on a whim, "Let's see if there's any property for sale."

As a child I had spent many summers in Bucks County on my grandparents' farm, and I had a great fondness for the area. The fact that I had no money to buy anything was irrelevant. I always feel that if you wait until you have the money to buy something, you'll never have it. There's *never* enough money.

So we drove out to my hometown, Easton, Pennsylvania, to find out what was happening in the area. From the looks of things, not much had happened in Easton for the past forty years. It's been in a state of depression ever since I left!

Easton's only claim to fame is that it's the home of Larry Holmes, the boxer. As we drove through town, Karl said to me drolly, "Do you think you'll ever become famous enough for them to call Easton the home of Larry Holmes and Sally Jessy Raphaël?"

"That would be nice," I said, "if they wanted to admit I was from there."

Apparently "they" didn't. When we walked into the musty Chamber of Commerce to inquire about sights to see in the area, the man behind the desk looked at me blankly.

"There's nothing much happening in this town—and never has been—except maybe Larry Holmes," said the man.

"Oh," said Karl. "I hear that Sally Jessy Raphaël also was born in Easton."

"I don't know who she is," he said. But he did know the name of a real estate agent, and he sent us over to meet her.

Although the real estate agent had no idea who I was either, she immediately set about trying to help us out. I told her we had a large family and were interested in a big house. She found just the thing in her real estate book: a bed-and-breakfast inn in nearby Erwinna.

She had never been to the place before, but following the instructions in her booklet, she drove down the road until we came upon a beautiful inn that seemed to be listed in her book at an unbelievably low price.

I knocked on the door, and a man said, "Can I help you?"

"Yes, we're here to see the place," I said.

He looked somewhat astonished, and I could tell by the surprised expression on his face that he recognized me.

But he didn't say anything about it, and I didn't bother to introduce myself. Instead, I started checking out every nook and cranny of his inn. I peeked in the closets, I measured some rooms, I checked out the kitchen, and I asked him about his appliances.

Finally, after forty-five minutes had passed, he cleared his throat and said politely, "Pardon me, do you mind if I ask what you're doing here?"

"We're interested in buying the place," I answered.

"It's not for sale," he said. "You must be looking for the one down the street."

"But why didn't you tell me this sooner?" I asked, astounded by his patience.

"What would *you* do," he said, "if Phil Donahue came to your house one day and asked to look around?"

That's what I call a true fan!

Sure enough, as my fan had said, just down the road was the inn we were looking for. It even had a name: The Isaac Stover House, an old Victorian place with eight rooms just waiting for guests to arrive. I bought it that very day and have fixed it up with so many drapes, satin pillows, and crystal chandeliers that it looks like a Victorian bordello.

Now we're in the bed-and-breakfast business, a pastime that dominates many of our weekends. Decorating the place was the easy part. Running the inn is another matter entirely. We learned the hard way that being an innkeeper is an exercise in self-restraint.

Before any guests arrived, I cautioned Karl, "Remember, we have to be discreet. *Never* ask for anybody's name!"

With that caveat in mind, we welcomed our very first guests, an elderly couple in their seventies. The minute they arrived, they sprinted spryly up the spiral staircase and checked into the all-white "honeymoon suite."

"Aren't they cute, Karl?" I whispered. "I bet they have a wonderful story to tell."

In the parlor later that night I decided to play the role of genial innkeeper and strike up a conversation.

"Are you having a wonderful weekend?" I asked cheerfully.

"Oh, yes," they said.

"You're such a sweet couple," I continued, "you must have wonderful stories to tell about your relationship. How long have you been married?"

At that the woman blushed, and the man started to stutter. "We-we're not married," he said.

I was so startled I lost all my composure. "Does this mean you're *shacking up?*" I shrieked.

The woman practically choked.

Later I said to Karl, "Isn't it just our luck? When we had the restaurant, a lady used the floor as a toilet. Now we have an inn, and the first people who check in are shacking up!

I realized then that I'd better confine my interviews to the television studio.

An Arresting Schedule: As you've probably gathered by now, it's hard for me to describe a day that's really "normal," either on weekends or during the week. More typical is the kind of high-wire juggling act I had to perform the day I *didn't* become Connecticut's Mother of the Year for 1988. At the time, the show was being taped in New Haven.

Every year the state of Connecticut singles out three mothers for special honor. There is usually an older woman, the kind who has eleven children and has raised them all while working full time, there's the mother who typifies the younger woman, and then there's the celebrity mother. In 1988 I was asked to be the celebrity mother.

I was very honored and was more than happy to try to accommodate the award ceremonies into my schedule of TV tapings. But in order to fit everything in, I was on a tight time schedule. I could make the breakfast at the governor's mansion in Hartford and would have just enough time to go to the State Capitol to receive my award in front of the legislature before I had to get to New Haven to tape the TV show.

I got all dressed up for the occasion in a lovely conservative suit. All the other mothers had on suits, too. It was very *Good Housekeeping* magazine, apple pie, Betty Crocker America. The other mothers and I met the governor's wife for breakfast, had a short press interview, and then were ushered to our limousines, which would take us to the State Capitol. Heading the motorcade was a motorcycle cop, followed by separate limousines carrying the governor's wife, me, the Senior Mother of the Year, and the Junior Mother of the Year. It was all very exciting, and as we sped along toward the Capitol, I thought how classy the state of Connecticut was to arrange such a spectacular event.

Before long, however, I looked out of the window of the limousine and discovered that somehow the limousine carrying the governor's wife was nowhere in sight. The next time I looked up there were two motorcycle cops flanking my limousine.

They were motioning us to come over and park.

"We must have arrived," I said to Karl as we pulled over to the side of the road.

Just at that moment a very large motorcycle policeman in a black leather jacket tapped on the window.

I rolled it down.

"Get out of the car," he said. "I'm writing you a ticket for making an illegal left-hand turn."

"Wait a minute," I said. "I'm Sally Jessy Raphaël."

The mention of my name meant absolutely nothing to him. There wasn't even a spark of recognition in his eyes.

I tried another tack. "I'm part of a motorcade," I said. "We're following a motorcycle policeman."

"Oh, yeah," he said. "I *am* a motorcycle policeman."

"No, no, you don't understand," I said with a sense of

urgency in my voice. "We're following one, and I'm on the way to becoming Mother of the Year."

"Sure, lady," he said, humoring me. "But you made an illegal left-hand turn."

"I didn't make any illegal left-hand turn. When you're in a motorcade following the governor's wife, you *can't* make an illegal turn."

He was not impressed. "I say it's illegal, and you are in trouble, and you're going to be in even more trouble. And all those other women, tell them to get out of their cars, too!" With that he motioned to his buddy to come over and help.

How could we get out of this one? We had two big motorcycle cops breathing down our necks, three Mothers of the Year with corsages on, and nothing I said could dissuade him from giving us a ticket.

"Please," I begged, "you can't do this. We're Mothers of the Year."

"Not only can't I, but I don't buy your story," he said. "Just because you've got corsages doesn't make you Mothers of the Year."

"I'm going to tell the governor," I said.

"You can tell anyone you want, lady," he said bluntly. "But if you say one more word, I'm going to arrest you."

With that Karl leaped out of the car and shouted, "Arrest her! Arrest her!"

I said to Karl, "Okay, enough of this. Grab a cab. The chauffeur will take the ticket."

By this time, though, it was too late for me to go to the legislature. I had just enough time to get to New Haven before my show was scheduled to start.

I wished the other two mothers well and sent them on their way to receive the awards without me.

I never did become Mother of the Year for the state of Connecticut. I never received the award, and no one ever called to ask what had happened to me.

The only thing I did get was the ticket. It came in the mail a few weeks later.

But in retrospect, I have to say that there is a sense of justice in the world. In 1989 I was again asked to be the Mother of the Year—this time by the National Mother's Day Committee. I went to a lovely luncheon in New York along with my daughters, Allison and Andrea. This time I got the award. Also, I didn't get a ticket.

There's one kind of ticket, though, that I'll never try to avoid: a plane ticket.

CHAPTER FIFTEEN

The World According
to Sally

IT DOESN'T TAKE MUCH to trigger my wanderlust.
All I need to hear is "Let's go to Cairo for the weekend,"
and in no time flat I'm suited up like Indiana Jones and
have my bags packed for adventure.

More often than not, the man behind these foreign
forays is our old pal Jay Van Vechten, who engineered the
"all-white picnic" back in our Miami days. These days,
when he's not running his Manhattan public relations
agency, he's dreaming up creative ways for all of us to get
away from it all.

The weekend in Cairo was one of those spur-of-the-
moment getaways that I couldn't turn down. A mutual
friend was having a birthday, and to celebrate, Jay suggested Cairo. At the time Karl had other plans, so he told
me to see enough of Egypt for the two of us. Coming
along for the ride was my friend Sandy Keay, the woman
who had once wandered the streets of Manhattan in a
futile search for my dog Fame.

Bright and early Friday morning I arrived at Jay's office
in full safari gear. I had on a pith helmet, khaki shorts and
vest, and sturdy shoes with enough rubber on the soles to
walk up the side of a pyramid. Even my luggage was khaki.

Since we were flying coach, we put together an extraordinary "bag lunch" so we could live like a pharaoh even if

we couldn't travel like one. We had purple plastic plates and lavender napkins, caviar, pâté, cold roast chicken, truffles, mandarin oranges, croissants, and cheese.

We were the envy of the entire airplane. Even first class didn't have it so good. But what made us stand out from the crowd wasn't really our food; it was my pith helmet, which I kept on for the entire trip. I wanted to hit the ground running when we landed, and we did indeed run!

Once in Egypt, we didn't stop for a second. We rode camels, took a trip down the Nile, saw belly dancers, and shopped in the bazaars for bizarre and unusual things. By Sunday night we were on our way back to New York exhausted but exhilarated.

To me, every road I travel is a road to adventure. Whether I'm tooling down the Missouri highway in a six-teen-wheel truck, heading down the Mae Kok in a flat-bottomed boat, or racing along Asian streets in a ricksha, I'm living out my wildest fantasies. The way I see it, the world is a giant theme park, just waiting for me to partake of its pleasures.

Over the years these real-life adventures have taught me not to be more cautious about life but, instead, to be willing to take even greater risks. The payoff is in the thrill I get pushing myself to new heights—and making it to the top. That's what makes me feel good about myself. That's what energizes my mind and spirit and makes me look forward to each and every day.

Once, when we were on vacation in Hawaii, I discovered that our hotel had a monumental water slide—a contraption that only the nine-year-old boys were brave enough to use. It went around and around endlessly, and from the top you couldn't see the bottom. I sat looking at it for two days before I got up the nerve to try.

With my heart thumping in my chest, I climbed to the top of the slide and then waved good-bye to Karl. Down I went, and when I reached the bottom, I turned around and went back for more. In those moments of exhilaration I felt as if I could accomplish *anything*—even conquer Mount Everest if I had to.

So that's why, no matter where I am in the world, I push myself to the limit, whether or not the odds are in my favor.

The odds definitely weren't in my favor in India the day Karl and I got to the airport in Udaipur. We were getting ready to board the plane when I decided to take a picture.

What I didn't know at the time was that someplace in the airport was a teeny-weeny sign that said NO PICTURES.

Needless to say, I didn't see any sign, so I happily pulled out my Pentax and snapped two pictures of Karl as he stepped into the plane.

Within seconds a huge, imposing Indian, outfitted in mufti with a gigantic purple turban, approached me threateningly. He looked exactly like Punjab of *Annie* fame, and I knew I was in trouble.

"Give me your camera," he said.

"What did I do wrong?" I answered back.

"I'm not telling you," he said. "Just give me your camera."

Now there's no way somebody is going to take my camera without telling me what's the matter, so I held my ground.

"You tell me what I did wrong, and then I'll give you my camera," I argued.

"I'm not telling you," he insisted.

By this time an enormous crowd had gathered on the tarmac. All the porters, the passengers, and the airport personnel were gathered in a circle around us, listening to every word.

Finally, in exasperation the Indian put the screws on: "If you don't give me that camera, you're under arrest."

Out of the corner of my eye, I could see one of his lackeys running to get more help. It flashed through my mind that I could be in really big trouble. "This Punjab look-alike is going to arrest me, and I'm going to be stuck in prison in Udaipur for the rest of my life," I thought. "I won't be able to do any more TV, I won't be able to give advice on radio, and I won't be able to spend my final days with my family."

Just as I began to think the worst, Karl came down the stairs from the plane to help.

"Go away," I said. "I'll handle it myself." By then he knew I was on to something.

I turned back to the officious Indian and continued to argue until he seemed ready to wring my neck. The look on his face told me that I was sheer dirt—not only American dirt but *female* American dirt —and I darned well better do what he said, or else.

By now my blood was boiling. "Nobody makes me feel bad about myself," I thought. All of a sudden I knew exactly what to do. My mind jumped back two weeks earlier, to a television show I had done on rape. The theme of the show had been "How females should protect themselves against rape if they're in an undesirable neighborhood."

It immediately clicked in my brain that I was in an "undesirable neighborhood." What's more, I was being raped verbally.

So I swung into action, using the techniques I had learned on my TV show. One of the things the rape expert had emphasized was that if you're ever in a state of desperation, act crazy.

That's exactly what I did. I started yelling and screaming at the top of my lungs, and to top it all off, I started singing "Dixie."

There, standing in the airport in Udaipur, eyeball to eyeball with Punjab, I was screeching, "Wish I was in the land of cotton, old times there are not forgotten." I ended with my own variation on the theme: *"Keep away, keep away, keep away, Dixie Land."*

With that the man drew back from me, and the crowd gasped, "Ahhhhhhhhhhh."

I knew I had him.

"Calm down, madam," he said. "Calm down."

Nobody would touch me. They were scared to death that they had a maniac on their hands, but they wouldn't put a finger on me. It must have been against their religion to touch a woman.

"All right, madam," he said as I continued to sing at the top of my voice.

"Let her get on the plane," he said to the crowd. "Move away so she can get on."

I continued to scream and sing all the way onto the plane. As I walked into the cabin, I could see that the seventeen other passengers were white with fright and dripping with perspiration from sitting so long in the heat.

Nobody said a word. But the minute Punjab left, I turned to Karl and grinned.

"How did I do?" I asked him.

"Great," he said. "But do me a favor. If this ever happens again, don't be an idiot. Give the man your camera."

"The camera's pretty important to me, Karl," I answered.

With that, I opened it up to take out the roll of film with the infamous pictures that had nearly sent me to jail.

The camera was empty. Punjab had gone through all that posturing for nothing.

But even without the pictures, I didn't come away empty-handed. I had taken a risk and pushed myself to the limit—and I had won.

Sometimes the payoffs I get from taking a risk aren't as immediate as they were that day in Udaipur. That's especially true when I've taken a gamble on a good cause. But I can safely say that whenever I've put my money where my heart was, I've never lost.

That's how I ended up adopting a group of hill tribesmen outside of Chiang Rai, Thailand, a few Christmases ago. Karl and I were on a Far Eastern junket with

Jay and our friend Michelle when somebody told us, "You've got to visit the Golden Triangle."

Up until then I had never had any desire to see the place that's considered the heart of heroin country. But when people tell me, "You really oughtta do this," I go, because they're usually right.

It turned out that the most adventurous way to get to Chiang Rai was by a very tortuous bus ride followed by an even more tortuous boat trip down the Mae Kok. It was a little like the jungle ride at Disney World, without the hippos.

Once we got there, though, what confronted us wasn't a band of thieving dope dealers living like kings, but a pitiful tribe of hill people who were barely eking out an existence. Their clothes—what they had of them—were badly torn, and they looked so poor and downtrodden that we immediately decided to take them under our wing.

"Let's adopt this tribe," we said to each other. We pooled the money we would have used for Christmas presents for each other, gave it to our guide, and asked her to buy them clothes when she had a chance.

You might think we were taking a chance, handing over several hundred dollars to a woman we would never see again. But at the time it seemed like the right thing to do. So we paddled back down the Mae Kok and forgot about the whole thing.

A month after we returned, Jay got a letter from a woman in New Zealand. She had just been on a trip up the Mae Kok and had come upon this unusual tribe of hill people. They all had identical blankets and were dressed alike in identical outfits from the Thai equivalent of Sears.

When the New Zealander inquired about this extraordinary sight, the guide told her that a month earlier four Americans had given her money to buy clothing for the whole tribe.

Enclosed in the letter was a picture of the tribe in their

spanking new clothes. In their hands was a sign saying THANK YOU.

The memories of that hill tribe and their new clothes added a special dimension to Chiang Rai. Our adventure in do-gooding transformed a visit to a depressing little village into an exciting and inspiring moment of sharing.

The truth about travel is that unless you seek out the unexpected, most places turn out to be somewhat of a disappointment. The world's sights and scenes are rarely as spectacular as the travel brochures say they will be.

What's more, there are lots of things in this world that we Americans take as a given but that aren't really true. I've discovered that you don't get French toast in France, and you don't find German potato salad in Germany. If they have them, they call them something else.

At no time in Germany did I ever meet anyone who had German measles. Up until recently there were no hamburgers in Hamburg, and if you ask for Spanish fly in Spain, no one has any idea what it is.

The French never had French fries until they learned our word for it. For them it was *pommes frites.* You don't go dutch in Holland because men would be terribly offended. Double dutch isn't called that if you're jumping rope in Holland. It's not possible to get a bowl of chili in Chile. The English don't know what we're talking about when we ask for an English muffin. And there are very few African queens.

I've never been to Russia; but a friend visited there and asked for Russian dressing, and the Russians don't have it. What's more, the Russians don't hang around playing Russian roulette. Most Turkish baths are closed, and when I tried to buy a Turkish towel in Turkey, people had no idea what I was talking about.

If my travels have taught me anything, it's that in order to make the world what you want it to be, you have to create adventures for yourself.

In Thailand, for example, the minute we stepped off the

boats that had taken us to Chiang Mai, we were met by several bicycle-driven rickshas. I said, "Everybody into a ricksha! Last one to the hotel pays for dinner!"

With that each of us jumped into a ricksha, and the race was on. "If you can get me to the hotel faster than those other rickshas, I'll double your money," I told the man pedaling my cart. We sped off in a cloud of dust.

Moments later the four rickshas, traveling at breakneck speed, converged on the hotel.

I don't even remember who won. But that's not the point. We all came out ahead that day because we shared in an experience of our own making. We took something as simple as a ricksha ride and turned it into an adventure in itself.

There is one place in the world, though, where you never have to worry about creating your own adventure. It's there for the asking. I'm talking about Nepal, high in the Himalayas.

We had started out from Nepal's capital, Kathmandu, ready for the thrill of a lifetime. Our destination was Tiger Tops, the famed game reserve that's a naturalist's dream. Set in the jungle in the middle of Nepal's Royal Chitwan National Park, Tiger Tops promised to be a close-hand look at nature at its most primitive. What we hoped to catch a glimpse of were herds of rhinos and, perhaps, even the rare Royal Bengal tiger.

The airplane—which left Kathmandu a day late because that's the way things work in Nepal—soared close to Everest and deposited us, and our luggage, in a dusty patch of ground on the edge of the jungle.

We had opted to stay safari-style in a rustic campsite in the park. But what we hadn't bargained for was that in order to get to the camp, we had to carry our luggage across endless miles of jungle terrain. A gap-toothed Nepalese man ferried us across a river to a spot surrounded by tall grass.

"Which way do we go?" I asked him.

"It doesn't matter," he answered, still smiling.

With that he took off in his boat and left the four of us standing in a marsh, wondering which way to turn.

"Let's get going," said Jay optimistically.

There was absolutely nothing in front of us except the merest hint of a path, but the four of us trudged along, lugging our luggage. If there ever was blind faith, this was it.

Finally, after interminable miles of walking, a man stepped out of the bushes to greet us.

He looked like one of those Japanese soldiers who were left behind on a deserted island in the Pacific after World War II.

"Does he know the war is over?" I said to Karl.

He directed us to our camp—a huge tent with cots and an outdoor campfire. The only amenities were a kerosene lamp and a bucket of water for each of us. The "toilet" was the jungle next door.

By the time we arrived, we were so exhausted that all we wanted to do was go to sleep. Karl checked under the beds to be sure no tigers had sneaked in, and we put down the flaps of the tent, zipped up the front, and got ready for bed.

Karl took off his clothes and promptly went to sleep. I went to bed fully dressed. I had on my pith helmet—the same helmet I had worn on the plane to Cairo—to protect me from the tigers. I had on my shoes—in case something dreadful happened and I had to run for help. I had on my red glasses—so I could see the tigers that were coming after us. And I had on my money belt—with all the money I had in the world. Karl may have been dead asleep, but one of us was going to be ready for trouble.

I must have fallen off to sleep because in the middle of the night I was awakened by snorting sounds.

"Karl!" I shouted. "Stop snoring!"

"I'm *not* snoring," he shouted back. "Be quiet and go to sleep."

"But I heard noises, Karl."

Ever the dutiful husband, Karl got up and checked the zipper of the tent to make sure we were safe and sound. Then he went back to bed.

The next morning I woke up, unzipped the zipper, and stepped out of the tent. There, on the ground, were enormous footprints. I'm no Indian guide, but I know an animal print when I see one. These looked like rhinos to me.

I ran to the first person I saw and said frantically, "There are rhinos."

"That's what you came to see," he said matter-of-factly.

I wanted to see rhinos, but I didn't want to see animals that looked like armored tanks right outside my tent!

"We'll take a ride out on the elephants and see them," said the guide.

"That sounds nice," I said. In my mind I imagined the elephant rides at the zoo—you know, ten minutes around the track and you're off the animal.

Well, four hours later, after swaying back and forth in our howdahs—the wooden seats on top of the elephants —we finally saw some rhinos. Whole herds of them.

The way I look at it, once you've seen one rhino, you've seen them all. By this time I had had enough of roughing it and was ready to get back to civilization.

But our safari experience wasn't quite over yet. At dawn the next day we were awakened for a boat ride to study some of the flora and fauna. Along with us were several of the students who were living at the campsite. There may not have been many tigers, but the place was crawling with biologists, botany students, and anthropologists from such places as Yale and the National Geographic Society, who were spending months at a time doing research.

As we rode along in the boat, we passed gorgeous birds that must have been rarer than the Bengal tigers. The zoologist next to me was practically having a heart attack with joy. "Faaabulous!" he exclaimed. "I haven't seen one of those."

Meanwhile, as he madly jotted down notes, I was busy swatting mosquitoes and wishing the whole thing were over. "My head hurts," I said. "I wanna get out of here.

"You know," I said to no one in particular, "I really belong in the Georges Cinq in Paris. I really don't belong in Nepal in a boat."

Once we got off the boat and got back to dry land, Nepal started looking good. From the air it looked even better. The nice thing about Royal Nepal Airlines is that the schedule and flight plan are so informal that you can make requests about the route.

"Do you mind if we fly over Everest so I can take pictures?" I asked the pilot.

The pilot didn't. He flew smack over Everest.

As I looked down on the world's highest mountain, which had challenged some of the century's most daring adventurers, I couldn't help thinking about my own struggles upward and the heights I had reached in my journey through broadcasting. There had been lots of slips and slides along the way. But ultimately I had made it to the top.

The first thing I did when we landed back in Kathmandu was turn to Karl, the guy who had been by my side through my long, circuitous journey to stardom.

There, on the steaming tarmac, I gave him a great big kiss. It was just like Bacall and Bogey—except that I was in my pith helmet and Karl was carrying the luggage.

Somehow that hot, sticky moment was symbolic of our lives: the long road we had traveled and the exciting roads we had ahead.

CHAPTER SIXTEEN

High Roll to Adventure

I SOMETIMES WONDER WHY I had to go the long way around.

Some people come on the broadcasting scene like gangbusters and never have even the hint of a struggle. With me, it was very different, but perhaps it was meant to be that way. Maybe I had some lessons to learn along the way to give me a perspective on fame and fortune and all those things I had always been yearning for.

At this point in my life I'm beginning to learn something about what fame and celebrity and success are all about. Over the years I've met the famous and the not-so-famous, and from those often chance encounters, I've distilled a few precious truths about what it means to be a success in this life.

From Jimmy Durante I learned what fame is *not*. I met Jimmy back in Puerto Rico when one of the hotels asked Karl and me to squire him around the old section of San Juan. We walked along the streets, pointing out the sights, and after about two hours Jimmy turned to me and said, "I gotta get out of this town."

"Why?" I said, puzzled.

"They don't know who I am," he answered. So he left town that very day and flew back to the States, where his famous schnoz was recognizable anywhere.

There are other celebrities, though, who might not stand out in a crowd but who give a very different meaning to the word "fame."

From Rod McKuen I learned what fame *can be*. When I was in Miami, desperately trying to make my mark in broadcasting, I decided that what I needed was to make a pilot of a show to send around to TV stations. My idea was to get a studio, recruit an audience, and get a star who would let his hair down during an interview.

But what famous person would take the time to do this for a virtual nobody in Florida? Who would bother to do a show that was never going to air?

Rod McKuen did it. At the time he was a big star who had brought poetry to the masses. Everybody was reading Rod McKuen's poetry and listening to his songs. I had interviewed him once before, so I got up my nerve and called him in California.

"I need the biggest favor," I said, explaining what I had in mind. Not only did he agree to come, but he paid his own way *and* that of his assistants for the trip to Miami.

He never asked for a thing in return—not even a copy of the tape!

Nobody did buy that pilot, and it ended up with the rest of my résumé items in a box of rejects.

I always wonder what happened to Rod McKuen. Over the years I've lost track of him, and I never knew what it was that sidetracked his career. What I do know is that in his heyday he was one heck of a celebrity.

What's more, he's still famous in my book, not because of who he was but because of what he did.

But perhaps what I've learned most in my years in broadcasting is that the key to success in life doesn't really have anything to do with fame at all. What counts is being a decent human being—whether you're famous or not.

Ironically, I learned that lesson from some of the toughest guys on the streets. One of them was an ex-con named Tony, who knows me from a different time and a different place.

Not long ago Karl picked up the phone and heard a voice from the distant past. "Karl, this is Tony," said the man with a thick Brooklyn accent.

"Tony!" Karl said. "Where've you been?"

"Well, I just been sprung," he said. "I was doin' some time, and I was studying law, and now I'm out. I caught Sally's show on television, and I wanted to let you know I'm thrilled for youse."

It had been more than twenty years since we had heard from Tony. The last time we had seen him was on the waterfront in San Juan, where we went to get money for Girl Scout uniforms to donate to an impoverished troop. Allison and Andrea were in a very fancy troop. Limousines transported the Scouts to campouts on the beaches, and butlers pulled out lobsters and steak instead of hot dogs for barbecues. But when we found out that another local troop was having trouble getting uniforms, we went searching for a benefactor.

"Who would be sure to give money to the Girl Scouts?" I asked Karl.

"The people who control the waterfront will always give money to anything that stands for God, mother, and country," said Karl.

"That sounds like what the Girl Scouts need," I said. "Let's go."

We put on makeshift uniforms and headed for the docks. Once there, we asked someone to direct us to the area's most notorious nightclub. We walked in brazenly, without a hint of trepidation.

"Can we see the owner?" we asked.

They led us into the back room, where a man said, "Yeah? Waddaya want?"

"Are you the owner of this establishment?" I asked.

"Yeah," he said.

"What's your name?" I asked.

"What's it to you?" he said.

"I'm just friendly," I answered. With that I introduced myself, and he told me his name was Tony.

Then I launched into my pitch. "Here's my problem, Tony," I said. "We need money for uniforms. Girl Scout uniforms."

"I beg your pardon?" he said.

There was a reason for Tony's surprise. It turned out he ran one of the biggest whorehouses in San Juan.

"Why should I give you money?" he asked.

"If the girls don't have uniforms, they don't feel good about themselves," I said. Just for emphasis, I added, "Scouting brings out the best in women. I'm sure you feel, as I do, that Scouting provides a great foundation for the women of America."

Now Tony was no psychologist, but he had a warm heart for a good cause. "It sounds good to me," he said. With that he pulled open a drawer filled with cash. There had to be twenty-five thousand dollars in cash in that drawer.

"How much do you need?" he asked.

"Gee, I don't know," I said. "Let me go home and put together a proposal and give it to you."

"You mean, you came in and you're asking me for money and you don't know how much you want?"

"I guess that's right," I said.

"Look," he says. "Let me give you some money, and I'll help you any way I can. You can always count on me."

He dipped into his drawer and handed me a wad of hundred-dollar bills.

"Don't you want a receipt from the Girl Scouts?" I asked.

"You must be kidding," said Tony. "With me a donation's a donation. I'm not like one of those creeps who gives money so he can take it off his income tax."

When we finally walked out into the sunshine, we found that the man had been overly generous. He had given us about seven hundred dollars. After we paid for the uniforms, we had enough money left over to give a hefty donation to the Scouts.

That was the last we heard from Tony until that phone call after his release from jail.

It's moments like these—filled with unexpected acts of kindness, often from people you least expect—that make life fun and endlessly fascinating.

Those moments don't add up to stardom. Nor do they always add up to big bucks. But they do add up to a rich store of love and generosity waiting for each of us to share.

If I've learned anything on this crazy journey of mine, it's that around every bend in the road, and at the end of even the darkest tunnel, there's likely to be a company of angels.

With me, though, they're more likely to be Hell's Angels!

A few years ago Karl and J.J. and I were in our van, traveling through Massachusetts to visit my cousins. It was very late, about two or three in the morning, when it became clear that we were lost. The country roads seemed to be going on forever, and the farther we traveled, the worse it seemed to get.

Finally we came upon one of those big granddaddy truck stops. So we pulled in for directions. Karl was really shot from all the driving, so I got out of the van to do the talking.

"Does anybody here know how to find Merridale Road?" I asked.

A very tired waitress looked up and said, "Lady, I haven't got a clue."

Since she wasn't going to be any help, I looked around at the customers. There, sitting nearby, were four of the toughest human beings I had ever seen in my life. Chains. Black leather. Skulls and crossbones. The whole bit.

I immediately thought of my family in the van and what these characters might do to us.

"We know where you're going," one of them said cheerfully. "Not only that, but we'll take you there."

Before I could say no, they got up off their chairs, paid their bill, and were outside on their motorcycles, gesturing "Follow us!"

We started to follow this large motorcycle gang down lonely Massachusetts country roads in the wee hours of the morning. There were four guys on motorcycles and four women who weighed three hundred pounds each sitting behind them.

After a few minutes J.J. decided it was all over for us. "They're taking us to a lonely spot, and that will be the end," he said ominously. "I'm never going to see my school or my friends again. How could you do this to me?"

I whispered to Karl, "I don't want to scare J.J. But he's right. I am a bit frightened. It's dark. The road is getting very lonely. And these people are tough. Maybe I did the wrong thing."

"No kidding," he retorted. "We're just going to have to trust that it's going to be all right."

"If they tell us to stop," I said, "don't stop. Gun the motor and keep going."

About an hour later, after winding through endless back roads deep in the woods, they motioned to us to go left.

We looked up, and there was the sign for Merridale Road. They had put us on the right road after all.

As they waved good-bye, I heard someone shout, "Keep up the good work, Sally!"

They had known who I was all along, yet they had never let on.

About six months later, when Burt was finishing the warm-up for the television show, I looked out in the studio audience and thought I saw an apparition.

There, sitting right smack in front of a bunch of proper Connecticut housewives, was the same motorcycle gang.

Burt took one look at the unsavory foursome and said aghast, "Do you see those people? What are we going to do?"

"Not only do I see them," I said, "but I know them." With that I took the mike and went over and renewed our friendship.

Ever since then, whenever I see or read anything about the Hell's Angels, I get a smile on my lips.

I remember how they once led me down the road—the long, unknown road to adventure. And how, at the end, I was treated to the biggest surprise of all.

That's how far fame has brought me. It's opened doors to the hearts of people: the famous and the infamous.

Through them I've found success. Unconventional success.

INDEX

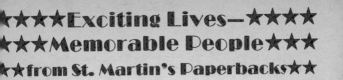

★★★★Exciting Lives—★★★★
★★Memorable People★★★
★★from St. Martin's Paperbacks★★

MAN OF THE HOUSE
"Tip" O'Neill with William Novak
_____ 91191-2 $4.95 U.S. _____ 91192-0 $5.95 Can.

CRISTY LANE: ONE DAY AT A TIME
Lee Stoller with Peter Chaney
_____ 90415-0 $4.50 U.S. _____ 90416-9 $5.50 Can.

THE MAN FROM LAKE WOBEGON
Michael Fedo
_____ 91295-1 $3.95 U.S. _____ 91297-8 $4.95 Can.

FROM THE HEART
June Carter Cash
_____ 91148-3 $3.50 U.S. _____ 91149-1 $4.50 Can.

DON JOHNSON
David Hershkovits
_____ 90165-8 $3.50 U.S. _____ 90166-6 $3.95 Can.

ISAK DINESEN
Judith Thurman
_____ 90202-6 $4.95 U.S. _____ 90203-4 $5.95 Can.

DENNIS QUAID
Gail Birnbaum
_____ 91247-1 $3.50 U.S. _____ 91249-8 $4.50 Can.

Publishers Book and Audio Mailing Service
P.O. Box 120159, Staten Island, NY 10312-0004
Please send me the book(s) I have checked above. I am enclosing $ _____ (please add $1.50 for the first book, and $.50 for each additional book to cover postage and handling. Send check or money order only—no CODs) or charge my VISA, MASTERCARD or AMERICAN EXPRESS card.

Card number _____

Expiration date _____ Signature_____

Name_____

Address_____

City_____ State/Zip_____
Please allow six weeks for delivery. Prices subject to change without notice. Payment in U.S. funds only. New York residents add applicable sales tax.

MP 1/89

Famous Lives

from St. Martin's Paperbacks

LIBERACE: THE TRUE STORY
Bob Thomas
_____ 91352-4 $3.95 U.S. _____ 91354-0 $4.95 Can.

THE FITZGERALDS AND THE KENNEDYS
Doris Kearns Goodwin
_____ 90933-0 $5.95 U.S. _____ 90934-9 $6.95 Can.

CAROLINE AND STEPHANIE
Susan Crimp and Patricia Burstein
_____ 91116-5 $3.50 U.S. _____ 91117-3 $4.50 Can.

PATRICK SWAYZE
Mitchell Krugel
_____ 91449-0 $3.50 U.S. _____ 91450-4 $4.50 Can.

YOUR CHEATIN' HEART:
A BIOGRAPHY OF HANK WILLIAMS
Chet Flippo
_____ 91400-8 $3.95 U.S. _____ 91401-6 $4.95 Can.

WHO'S SORRY NOW?
Connie Francis
_____ 90386-3 $3.95 U.S. _____ 90383-9 $4.95 Can.